PRAISE FOR *101 LESSONS FROM THE DUGOUT*

"This book has everything for young ballplayers and fans alike—life lessons, love of sports, and a genuine passion for the games of baseball and softball. It's easy for me to see the tremendous value of these lessons because I was really born and bred in baseball. There couldn't be a better set of guidelines for life, period, no matter what age you are. The authors have captured the essence of baseball and softball and, in so doing, have captured the essence of life off the diamond, as well. This is a book that needs to be on the shelf of every young player and fan, every coach, and every school library."

—**Reggie Jackson**, Hall of Fame baseball player

"Through all my years playing baseball, I knew I learned a ton of life's lessons, whether it was perseverance, hard work, communication, how to handle failure, or fighting for a spot. But I didn't really realize until I started to read this book just how many things I actually did learn. What I love about *101 Lessons from the Dugout* is that it applies to all ages—anyone could read this book and get a lot out of it. And I think there's life lessons for an adult like myself to read and teach to my kids. Coaches can use it, too. The lessons to be learned from baseball and softball are endless, and this book displays them beautifully. I think it's brilliant."

—**Joe Girardi**, World Series-winning Yankees manager and player

"As a coach and ultimately an educator, I have always believed that the greatest purpose of sports is to teach young people LIFE. In *101 Lessons from the Dugout*, authors Harley Rotbart and Ken Davidoff uniquely break down America's greatest games, baseball and softball, and analogize each moment to the game of life. This book is a wonderful, insightful look at our beloved sports and how we can apply them to the opportunities we have in our daily lives."

—**Carol Hutchins**, winningest softball coach in NCAA history

"It's always been said that the game of baseball parallels the history of our great nation. Perhaps . . . but what Harley Rotbart and Ken Davidoff have accomplished is to thoughtfully demonstrate that baseball actually is a parallel and reflection of all our lives. In this book, the authors masterfully break down the complicated game of baseball into simplified life lessons that, when followed, transcend balls and strikes, hits and errors, and wins and losses."

—**Bernie Williams**, legendary New York Yankees outfielder

"This book has home run written all over it. Rotbart and Davidoff are masterful writers and the baseball metaphors are brilliant. They have turned baseball and softball into a philosophy of life and a guidepost for the healthy development of young adults. Every parent will want to give their baseball and softball players a copy of *101 Lessons from the Dugout*."

—**Barton D. Schmitt**, MD, Professor Emeritus of Pediatrics, University of Colorado School of Medicine, and international bestselling author of *Your Child's Health* and *My Child is Sick!*

"I didn't understand why colleges like to see sports on an application until I became the parent of a student athlete. I saw the discipline required for my son to balance school and lacrosse. I watched the life lessons learned, both on and off the field. It didn't matter that he would never go pro—it wasn't about that. As Rotbart and Davidoff so brilliantly point out, it's about how sports can shape the person our children will become. Not allowing batting order to define you; understanding when to be a team player and when to be a team leader; the importance of tuning out negative chatter— the life connections made by the authors make this book a must-read for players, coaches, and parents."

—Meredith Jacobs, author of the bestselling parenting journal series, "Just Between Us"

Special Praise for Author Ken Davidoff

"I've always looked at Ken Davidoff as a person who cares about the game and cares about the people he wrote about. For me, Kenny took an interest in the player, the game, how it was supposed to be played, and how it was supposed to be reported to the fan. I've always respected Ken's work because of who he is and who he has been to me. I did enjoy talking to several people in the press because they made sense and could hold good conversations. Kenny was at the top of the list. Enjoy the book, everyone—I certainly have!"

—Reggie Jackson ("Mr. October")

101 LESSONS FROM THE DUGOUT

What Baseball and Softball Can Teach Us About the Game of Life

HARLEY A. ROTBART, MD
KEN DAVIDOFF

FOREWORD BY DAVID WRIGHT

BLOOMSBURY ACADEMIC
NEW YORK · LONDON · OXFORD · NEW DELHI · SYDNEY

BLOOMSBURY ACADEMIC
Bloomsbury Publishing Inc, 1359 Broadway, New York, NY 10018, USA
Bloomsbury Publishing Plc, 50 Bedford Square, London, WC1B 3DP, UK
Bloomsbury Publishing Ireland, 29 Earlsfort Terrace, Dublin 2, D02 AY28, Ireland

BLOOMSBURY, BLOOMSBURY ACADEMIC and the Diana logo are trademarks of
Bloomsbury Publishing Plc

First published in the United States of America, 2026

Cover design: Devin Watson
Cover image: © istock/CNuisin

Library of Congress Cataloging-in-Publication Data

Names: Rotbart, Harley A. author | Davidoff, Ken author
Title: 101 lessons from the dugout : what baseball and softball
can teach us about the game of life / Harley A. Rotbart and
Ken Davidoff ; Foreword by David Wright.
Other titles: One hundred and one lessons from the dugout
Description: New York : Bloomsbury Academic, 2026. |
Includes bibliographical references and index. | Audience: Ages 12-22
Identifiers: LCCN 2025027870 (print) | LCCN 2025027871 (ebook) |
ISBN 9798765163009 paperback | ISBN 9798765163023 epdf |
ISBN 9798765163016 epub
Subjects: LCSH: Baseball–Philosophy–Juvenile literature |
Softball–Philosophy–Juvenile literature | Conduct of life–Juvenile literature
Classification: LCC GV867.5 .R68 2026 (print) | LCC GV867.5 (ebook) |
DDC 796.35709–dc23/eng/20250805
LC record available at https://lccn.loc.gov/2025027870
LC ebook record available at https://lccn.loc.gov/2025027871

ISBN: PB: 979-8-7651-6300-9
ePDF: 979-8-7651-6302-3
eBook: 979-8-7651-6301-6

Typeset by Deanta Global Publishing Services, Chennai, India

For product safety related questions contact productsafety@bloomsbury.com.

To find out more about our authors and books visit www.bloomsbury.com
and sign up for our newsletters.

To my Kids' Kids: G, J, M, T, L, S, and O—H.R.
To Mom, Sarah, and JJ. And, of course, to Dad—K.D.

CONTENTS

CONTENTS

FOREWORD

One afternoon last year, my younger daughter, Madison, came home from school in tears. She had just gotten back a math test, and the score crushed her. Not just because she wanted to do better, but because she thought she had let her mom and me down.

Madison needed a pep talk—and a strategy to get better at math.

I sat down with her and said, "You know how with your soccer team, you have two practices a week, and how the more you practice, the better you get?"

"Yeah," she nodded, still sniffling.

"And in softball, when we go to the batting cages, the more I pitch to you, the better you start hitting, right?"

"Yeah," Madison nodded.

"Well, math is the same thing," I told her. "Let's spend thirty minutes a day working through your math problems and I bet you'll get better at it."

Her face lit up. "So you mean if I work harder and practice at *anything*, I'll get better at it? Even math?"

This was the lightbulb moment. "Exactly," I said. "Just like softball. Or soccer."

We practiced, and sure enough, she improved. What seemed like common sense to me was a huge realization for her. And it hit me—I learned the same lesson when I was her age. But instead of softball or soccer, it was baseball that taught me.

My father Rhon, a police officer in Norfolk, Virginia, bought me a glove, bat, and ball before I even came home from the hospital. At home, my dad and my mom, Elisa, who drove our school bus, raised me and my three younger brothers with some simple but important rules: shake hands, look people in the eye, treat people fairly, and be on time, just for starters.

And then there was Coach Marvin "Towny" Townsend, who ran a baseball camp at the nearby Greenbrier Christian Academy around the time I hit Little League age. He was one of the first people who really made me think about how baseball connects to the rest of life.

Towny didn't teach baseball like most coaches. In addition to using actual baseballs, he would collect the plastic lids of coffee cans and Cool Whip containers, and frisbee them at us while we stood at home plate with our bats. We'd see who could hit the most in a row, all for a piece of gum as a prize. We would also work on memorizing the poem "Casey at the Bat" before and after every practice. I still can recite it to this day.

It didn't feel like "just" practice. It felt like a fun day in the park—with benefits! The benefits were what Towny taught us besides baseball skills. Towny was teaching us about life. He'd start talking about the fundamentals of baseball, and then all of a sudden he would start connecting it to our schoolwork, or doing our chores, or about how to treat people. His fellow coach Allan Erbe, a master at helping us with our fielding, also connected baseball to life in the same wise and gentle way. At first, I thought, what does baseball have to do with my grades? Or doing my chores?

It wasn't until high school that I finally got it. The way you work hard on the field is the same as the way you work hard in school. The way you support your teammates is the same as the way you support people in your community. And the way you handle a tough loss is the same way you handle tough times in general.

These lessons stayed with me throughout my fifteen seasons in Major League Baseball. And now, I try to pass them down as a coach, and as a dad to Madison, her older sister Olivia, and her little brother Brooks. I promised I'd coach each of them in one sport, so now I coach Olivia's soccer team, Madison's softball team, and Brooks's baseball team.

Sadly, Towny passed away in 2007, but I try to honor his memory in how I coach. We do our share of traditional drills, but sometimes, to mix it up I take my players and their parents to the beach for wiffle ball games. On really hot days, we hit water balloons instead of baseballs. Because when you're having fun, you don't even realize you're learning something bigger.

I hope you're having fun when you play sports, and that you realize you just might be learning more than you think! Baseball and softball are full of life lessons: practice makes you better, whether you're adding two fractions or batting with two strikes; be careful, whether you're running the bases or making decisions in life; being a good friend is just as important as being a good teammate.

That's why I love the 101 lessons in Harley Rotbart and Ken Davidoff's book—they connect the small details of baseball and softball to the big lessons in life. I'm using it for my teams, and I hope you will too.

Because in the end, the dugout is more than just a bench. It's where you learn the lessons that stick with you for the rest of your life.

*–**David Wright** is the New York Mets' all-time leader in hits (1,777), runs batted in (970), runs scored (949), and doubles (390). He served as the Mets' team captain from 2013 until his retirement after the 2018 season. His autobiography,* The Captain, *came out in 2020. He lives in Manhattan Beach, California with his wife Molly and their children Olivia, Madison, and Brooks.*

ACKNOWLEDGMENTS

The authors are grateful to Lisa Leshne of the Leshne Agency for her support and guidance during the preparation and "pitching" of this book. Many thanks, also, to Christen Karniski and Joanna Wattenberg at Bloomsbury Publishing, for believing in the value sports have for kids' lives off the fields—and believing in our ability to convey that value. We are so grateful to the amazing David Wright for buying into our vision and supporting it with his platinum-brand credibility, and to New York Mets media-relations guru and all-around superstar Jay Horwitz for his facilitating and cheerleading.

We are especially grateful to our wives, Sara Rotbart and Sarah Davidoff, who have supported us during the many hours of writing, editing, re-writing, and re-editing, and who have taught our kids the value of having fun whether winning or losing the game.

And to our own kids—Samantha, Sam, Eitan, Emily, Nurit, Matt, and JJ—who have taught us more than we could ever teach them.

Introduction

Congratulations! You are players and fans of the greatest games on Earth. You may not realize it yet, but as baseball and softball experts, you have acquired unique insight into the secrets for a happy and successful life. If you're a player, you are among the nearly 35 million in the United States who play youth baseball or softball and have already learned hidden truths from the oracle of the diamond. But they are well-hidden truths, and you may not even have noticed your enlightenment. Being a kid is like being in the "on-deck circle" of life, waiting for your turn to be an adult. What you learn now "on deck" will help you when you're up to bat as an adult in the real world. And we think you may learn so much about life by comparing it to baseball and softball that you'll even be able to teach your parents a few things when they face some rough spots in their lives.

101 Lessons from the Dugout is a book of wisdom for life disguised as a baseball and softball book. It's written for young adults like you, but we believe your parents and coaches and other adults in your life will find these lessons to be as relevant for them as they are for you. So they should read it, too.

The format of *101 Lessons from the Dugout* is simple. It is a collection of 101 of the most fundamental aspects of baseball and softball, presented in short and simple summaries at the top of each brief chapter. You already know about all of these: the strikeout, the walk, the sacrifice, the pickle, the hit and run, base stealing, the double play, and many others. We use these fundamentals of the games to teach the real-world messages and meanings you need to learn to be successful off the field. Lessons about self-esteem, courage, gratitude, resilience, sympathy, and patience. These are the keys to your future happiness and success in the major leagues of school, friendships, and family life.

You may think you know all there is to know about baseball and softball. And you certainly do know the rules and the strategy because you use them in every practice and game. But there are important life lessons underlying the rules and strategy. For example, you already understand how to "wait for the right pitch," "take a bigger lead," "tag up," "lay one down," and "call it on a pop fly." *101 Lessons* teaches that those fundamentals of the *sport* hold important clues to the fundamentals of *life*. Picking the right pitch to swing at is the ultimate exercise of good judgment and common sense; a runner leading off a base perfectly demonstrates the balance of risk and reward; the self-discipline of tagging up rather than running with the crack of the bat is true impulse control; bunting shows the value of sacrificing for others; and calling for the pop fly asserts leadership and accepts responsibility.

101 Lessons is a book of wisdom for life, drawn from the everyday, every-play circumstances of the diamond. Hope you enjoy the book. Now . . . Play Ball!

Note for Parents and Coaches

Our goal in writing this book—Harley as a pediatrician and parenting writer, Ken as a baseball writer, and both of us as parents and former youth baseball coaches—is simply to put you and your kids in the same space as often as possible and for as long as possible. When that space is made more fun, vivid, and vibrant by a shared love of baseball and softball, the time you spend together becomes even more meaningful and memorable. Talk with your kids and players about their games and the plays that stood out for them, and then easily find those plays among the 101 lessons in this book to further enhance the experience you are sharing with them.

The key words are "together" and "sharing." Your kids and players will remember the messages about life they learned from the games they love, but even more importantly, they'll always remember you were there with them, in their dugout and on their team.

PART I

IN THE DUGOUT

1

Keeping Score

Give 110 Percent
Self-Respect

Legendary players, legendary games, legendary moments. Legendary means famous, fantastic, something that will be remembered for a long, long time. The many details of baseball and softball games are officially recorded in the scorebook, where each event on the field has its own special symbol. At the end of each game and each season, the accomplishments and performances of each player can be counted, averaged, summarized, and analyzed. The exact number and types of hits and outs. How many pitches a pitcher threw and how many for strikes. Whether the groundout was hit to the third baseman or to the shortstop. Much more important, though, is what's *not* written in the scorebook—the spirit and soul of the at-bat, the cleverness and courage of the pitcher, the hustle and heroics of the fielders. Storybook performances are recorded in the hearts and minds of the players, coaches, and fans. A caught fly ball in the scorebook is just that and only that, whether it was a routine pop-up or a running, diving, acrobatic catch at the fence. But brilliant plays and dazzling efforts *are* scored and stored—in the memories of everyone who saw them.

You are much more than just a list of your accomplishments. It's not only *what* you do, but *how* you do it that counts in the scorebook of your life. Making the spectacular, diving catch says much more about you than the simple "out" that is recorded in the scorebook. It says you have game. It says you give *110 percent.* Every "fly ball" in your life off the field becomes a choice you must make. Will you do just enough to get by, maybe even letting the ball drop in front of you for a hit? Or will you push yourself to perform like a Hall of Famer and dive for the ball?

Your special effort will be recorded in the minds and memories of others, but going for it will do more than just gain the respect of your friends and fans. You will earn the *self-respect* and peace of mind that come from knowing you gave your very best—even if you don't end up making the catch. That's the stuff of legends.

2

The Starting Lineup

Prove You're Ready
Earn Your Spot
Believe in Yourself

Baseball and softball starting lineups call for nine players, which for many teams means almost as many players will be sitting on the bench when the game starts. That's the reality of life on the diamond. But those players who are not starting can also make important contributions—by cheering for their teammates, following the game, keeping the scorebook, and helping with the equipment. And they must be ready to go into the game when the coach calls them.

Life off the field also often has more players for opportunities than there are starting roles. Only a few can be "first chairs" in the school orchestra, leads in the school play, soloists in the choir, and winners of the student council election. If you're named a starter in any of life's games, be proud and grateful—and humble, too. Don't assume you'll always be a starter. Keep earning your spot. Perform like a starter: hustle; improve your skills; be gracious and never gloat. Remember you are part of a team.

And when life *doesn't* put you in the starting lineup? Perform like a starter, anyway, in whatever role you're assigned. Your day will come, even if it's not in this game or in this season. Keep practicing, learn from watching others, ask questions. Prove to those around you, and to yourself, that you're ready to come into the game when called.

Don't judge yourself through the eyes of others. Regardless of whether this coach or the next doesn't consider you a starter, you should always see yourself as one. Others' opinions of your abilities and potential may be way off; you know yourself better than anyone else knows you. Rejections are part of life. They may come from coaches, teachers, social media "friends," and even real friends. The only rejection you should *never* experience is from yourself. Believe in yourself because you *are* a starter, whether you find yourself on the field or on the bench for this one game.

3

Playing Time

The Right Attitude
When Life Is Unfair
Speak Up for Yourself

A mysterious formula explains how much time the coach lets each player play. The equation involves Some combination of A's: Ability, Age, Attendance, and Attitude; add Academics for school teams. What varies from coach to coach is how much value they put on each of the A's. Some coaches go with ability—the best players play the most. Other coaches reward a positive attitude and perfect attendance more than they do pure baseball and softball skills. Some coaches give the older players more time because the younger ones will be back next season.

There is more than one way to earn your spot and increase your playing time on any team. What qualifies you to play in life's games is a combination of your actual skills and harder-to-measure things like attitude, how hard you work, and team spirit. Your energy, enthusiasm, and commitment affect the decisions people make about you. If you pout and sulk, your chances of getting more playing time will go down.

Unfortunately, how much you play may not seem to make sense. In life, there isn't always a good reason for the way you are treated, and you often can't control it. What you can control is your effort, trying your hardest, and being the best you can be. In most cases, it will pay off—you'll play more and be more successful. But sometimes life is unfair. Take comfort in knowing you've done everything you can. Move on and hope fate plays more fairly the next time.

It's okay to question your playing time if you do it politely and respectfully. "Coach, it's not fair! I'm as good as the kids you put in the lineup, and work twice as hard, but they get to play more than me" isn't polite *or* respectful. "Coach, what do I need to do to get in the game more? I'll work harder, come earlier to practice for extra batting or fielding drills, whatever it takes!" is both polite *and* respectful. It also can remind the coach that you're not playing a lot. Remember, coaches are human—they may have lost track of your time on the field. Asking politely and respectfully gives you another chance to show your positive attitude, which could gently push the coach to think again about your playing time and maybe even feel a little guilty about it, which is not a bad thing.

The same strategy can also work with your teachers and, yes, even your parents (being polite and respectful is especially important when you question your parents' decisions!). Even if this polite and respectful approach to questioning the important people in your life doesn't lead to more playing time, or better grades, or fewer chores at home, your discussion will give you a better idea about how the decisions were made—and may really give you an idea of what more you *can* do.

4

Batting Order

Labels People Give You
Adjusting to a New Role

There's a lot of fable and foolishness involved in the batting order. What we think of the leadoff hitter is much different from how we think of the "clean-up" hitter (fourth to hit), and both are completely different from how we picture the batter hitting ninth. Coaches talk about "classic number two" and "classic number three" hitters (those hitting second and third in the batting order). Speed, strength, consistency, and other hard-to-measure stuff all go into the coach's decision about who bats when. Really, though, it only matters for the first inning, until the first three outs are made by the hitting team. After that, any batter might lead off an inning; any batter might come up with runners in scoring position. Hits are just as important for number eight batters as they are for leadoff hitters. But batting order labels can affect how players feel about themselves and even how they perform. Batters in the number two, three, and four spots think of themselves as the best hitters while batters hitting eight and nine think of themselves as the worst. The number seven batter may feel less important to the team than the number six hitter.

You're only a number nine hitter if you believe the label and start to think like a number nine hitter. As you play through the innings of your life, you determine your own success at the plate, regardless of how you are labeled by others. And you *will* be labeled by others. "Fast group" in reading, "slow group" in math, "gifted and talented," "learning-challenged," "honor roll," "class clown," "geek," "dumb jock," "troublemaker," "born leader," "follower." If someone brands you a number nine hitter in any part of your life, don't fall for it. Ignore the labels. Play every game the best you can, no matter what the expectations are of those around you.

Positive labels can have negative effects, too. Good hitters who have been batting eighth may suddenly slump when they're named the new leadoff or clean-up hitter. Expectations come with the title, and the pressure of those expectations can be great. Whatever someone else calls you, you are still you. Your coach or your teacher may believe that by rewarding you with a new position, you will magically find new abilities to fill that role. You may start to believe that, too. The combined weight of others' expectations—and your own—may make you slump and fail. A new title or label means your performance *up until now* has been noticed and appreciated, and you have promise for even better in the future. It does not mean you will immediately become that new label. Give yourself time to grow into a new role. Expect a lot from yourself but be reasonable—you can't make it to the Hall of Fame in a day. The skills and mindset that earned your new label will continue to carry you as you develop into your new spot in the batting order.

5

The Uniform

Standing Out
Blending In
Acting Cool

Game day holds a special elegance because baseball and softball require strict dress codes. At practices, players may look shabby, shaggy, and different than their teammates. On game day, though, teams wear crisp, matching uniforms, dressed the same down to their socks and belts. Hats are turned with their brims facing front. Cleats are good, sneakers bad. Umpires strictly enforce the rules: helmets on the hitting team; jerseys tucked into pants; watches, jewelry, and other distractions stay in the dugout. The uniform raises the performance of the team, bringing it a greater sense of togetherness and importance.

There is a time to be an individual and a time to blend in. Calling attention to yourself during a team effort takes away from your teammates and from your team. Face paint on class picture day, torn jeans at church, or a tie-dyed T-shirt and shorts at the speech meet will certainly get you noticed, but for the wrong reasons. When everyone is focusing on you, your team loses its unity and dignity.

When you show off, trying to look cool, you are really showing off how un-cool you are.

Cool people are quietly self-confident. That gets you noticed for the right reasons. Stand out by your play, your hustle, and your positive attitude, not by wrong behavior or wrong clothes in the wrong places at the wrong times. When the game is over, tear off your uniform and cleats and become the individual you are. But during the game, at school, at your music recitals, or in church, wear the uniform that fits the setting, and blend in for the good of the team.

Some fun with uniforms can be a good thing, but only if everyone on the team, including the coach, is in on it. Differently colored shoelaces on your cleats or little messages on your caps that are unique to you, but part of a team scheme, can strengthen team spirit while still letting you express yourself as an individual. The same is true for your off-the-field teams. The face paint may fit in as part of a team effort on "Spirit Day" at school. Torn jeans are probably fine for Field Day. And a tie-dyed T-shirt and shorts are perfect for your summer volleyball league in the park.

6

Equipment

Find Real Value
Appreciate What You Have

Since the discovery of fire and the invention of the wheel, we have known the right tools improve both the product and the performance. Baseball and softball tools keep getting more complicated—and more expensive. Different gloves are designed for catchers, first base, infielders, and outfielders. Bats are made with precious metals, each more rare and mysterious-sounding than the one before. Every year brings fancier equipment: the latest bat is guaranteed to give more "pop," the newest glove designed for a "truer pocket" and "easier snap." When a teammate shows up with this year's hot and expensive new item, the dugout buzzes. Every player needs to hold it, try it out.

Why should baseball and softball gear be different from equipment for the rest of life, where each new and more expensive gadget adds clearer pictures, truer sound, or cooler graphics? But when you judge an item's value by how "cool" it is, how many kids are using it, or how much it cost, you might forget what's truly valuable. How much "pop" does a bat need to hit the ball well? Watch what happens when all your teammates try out the new titanium weapon. Yes, the strong hitters may hit the ball a little farther with the super-bats, but those hitters led the team with their old bats, too. The medium hitters continue to hit medium—maybe the ball comes off the bat a little harder, maybe not. The outcome of their season doesn't change, and average players don't become superstars by changing equipment. Great photographers will take great pictures with a great camera; they will also take great pictures with a good camera. A concert pianist will sound fabulous on a Steinway Grand but will sound almost as fabulous on the well-tuned upright piano. How much better is the newest version of a cell phone, video game, or game console, and is it worth the cost of the "upgrade"? As a hitter, you get better by practicing, training, and conditioning. Your swing, not what you are swinging, is what's most important in how hard and how far the ball is hit. The next time a new piece of equipment shows up in your dugout, or in your friend's house, remember this year's hot new thing will be next year's old news. But the basic values and skills you develop will carry over from one season to the next.

More may be less. Sometimes new and fancy equipment can even make your performance *worse*. The weight and balance of a new bat may not be as comfortable for you as your old bat. The specialized glove for first base, with its extra-long shape, increased webbing, and deeper pocket, may cause fielding and catching errors you never would have made with your familiar old fielder's mitt. Appreciate what you have. New isn't always better; expensive isn't always best.

7

Pinch Hitters and Pinch Runners

Include Others
Speak Up for Friends

During the game, eager and anxious players wait on the dugout bench for their turn to get in and play. Substitutions in the middle of a game are common. Coaches put in a good hitter or fast runner at an important moment and try to make sure everyone gets some playing time before the last out. Players who hit better than they field can be a big help off the bench as pinch hitters. The player who doesn't hit *or* field well may run fast, and a good pinch runner can also make an important contribution to a team.

Even though you would rather play than sit while others are in the game, you should still feel bad when a teammate doesn't get into the game at all. When your friend doesn't have a chance to participate, it changes the feeling on the team—a loss is harder to take, and a win is less exciting. Imagine yourself as the one who sits on the bench the whole game. How would you feel? Life is full of chances to keep people out. From school clubs and cliques to birthday parties and sleepovers, there are always those whom others would keep out. When it's up to you, include, don't exclude. You'll feel better, the others will feel better, and the group will perform better.

It may be tempting to follow the "cool crowd" who find you worthy but enjoy keeping others out. Don't join them. Speak up for the outsiders—and consider whether you really want to be part of a crowd that acts that way to your other friends. The same group may change its mind about you someday. Every game can use a pinch runner or a pinch hitter, and every player off the bench becomes part of the team effort, making everyone stronger and raising the spirit in the dugout.

8

On Deck

Prepare in Advance
Learn from Those Ahead of You

The greatest chance during a game for instant learning and preparation comes when a batter is "on deck." The next player up to bat is allowed out of the dugout and onto the field to stand in a specially marked spot, the "on-deck circle," with an up-close view of the pitcher and the action at home plate. Being on deck gives players an important look ahead at what the immediate future holds for them. Pitchers' motions, emotions, and habits—as well as the types and speed of their pitches—are all on display for players paying close attention in the on-deck circle. They also get a good look at the umpires and the boundaries of their strike zone.

Prepare in advance, however it works best for you. In baseball and softball, that may mean focusing on the details: stand like a batter, take a practice swing with each pitch, time your swing to the pitcher's delivery. For other players, the on-deck circle is a place to relax and take some deep breaths ahead of the challenges to come. Your time on deck is valuable—make the most of it. There are on-deck circles available for you in almost every activity off the field, as well. Prepare in advance for school exams, musical performances, debate and speech meets, interviews for after-school jobs, and, when that big day arrives, your driving test! As the old saying goes . . . prior proper planning prevents poor performance.

Sometimes life gives you a close-up preview of the challenges about to come your way. Your good friend one grade up knows about the teachers you'll have next year and how strict they are with homework assignments. Your older sister gets grounded for missing curfew. A classmate gets sent home from school for a dress code violation. Learn from those ahead of you and around you—this is your crystal ball (crystal baseball!), a chance to know the unknown. Whenever you're allowed on deck—in school, at home, or with friends—with a chance to learn from those ahead of you and around you, use it as a heads-up and a head start. The reason the on-deck circle is so close to the batter is because the view is better there than anywhere else on the field. A better view means a clearer focus of what's going on. Get a good view of what's going on all around you. If you're daydreaming or fooling around in life's on-deck circles, you've missed a chance to do better when it's your turn.

PART II

AT THE PLATE

9

The Batter's Box

Your Comfort Zone
Arrive Early
You Are the Right Person

The chalk lines around baseball and softball diamonds come together at the small space surrounding home plate where the batter stands to face the pitcher. That space is the batter's box. When the batter is in the box, the pitcher can throw the ball; when the batter steps out of the box, the pitcher waits. Batters form a plan each time they step into the box. For slow pitchers, the batter stands up in the box, as close to the front as possible; if the pitcher is fast, the batter moves back in the box, furthest away, to allow the most time to react to the pitch. Some hitters "crowd," inching as close to the plate as they can, giving them better reach for the outside corner; others stand further away, either by habit or because they're afraid of being hit by the pitch. It's inside these few square inches of dirt that batters put themselves into their comfort zone at the plate, the best position to face the pitcher for the one-on-one battle only one of them can win.

The different spots in the batter's box are only a matter of inches apart, but the effect of moving an inch or two can be great in how comfortable you feel as a batter—and can help you succeed. Small moves in life's other batter's boxes can also make a big difference in what you're able to do or how comfortable you are doing it. When you're "up to the plate" for a big project, dress the part in your favorite clothes, the ones that make you feel comfortable, confident, and proud. If red is your "power color," wear a neatly pressed red shirt or dress for your interview. Pick the quietest, calmest place in your home, the room and desk where you can settle in most comfortably, to do your homework. Schedule your activities in a way that lets you get from one to the other with enough time to spare so you can find your comfort zone when you arrive for each. And don't overschedule so you can be your very best when it counts the most.

One of the best ways to get comfortable in life's batter's boxes off the field is to get into them early. Rushing in at the last minute before class, a test, a practice, or a performance doesn't let you get comfortable in the box. It throws you off your game plan and makes it harder to find the best position to get a hit. But when you get there early, you have enough time to pick a good seat, find what you'll need to do, get a drink of water and, finally, settle in for the "pitch." Now you're ready!

When you step into the batter's box, it's as if you're the only person in the game; even if there are eight other players who are better hitters, it's now up to you. You have to "step up to the plate," right then. There are many situations in life when you, and only you, must step up, take charge, lead. Whenever you have the opportunity at school, at home, or in the community, be ready. You should really want the chance to take charge and really believe you can do it. Preparing ahead of time and taking lots of practice are good ways to be ready. But really *wanting* the chance and *believing* in yourself come from deep inside you. Before you're up to bat in any of life's batter's boxes, be the person who can't wait to step into the box. When you're at bat, stare down the pitcher and any challenge you are facing, and go to battle. And, as soon as this at-bat is finished, start looking forward to your next one. You are the right person, at the right time. *Believe* you can face any challenge, any time, and *want* to face that challenge. You are in the batter's box, right where you belong.

10

Chatter

Block Out the Noise
Gossip

Baseball and softball games are noisy places. Fans are cheering, coaches are yelling, and players are shouting support to their teammates. There's often another kind of noise as well. There are still teams that "chatter," taunting the other team's batter, or pitcher, or fielder in a mean way. Yelling "Hey batter, batter, swing!" or "We want a pitcher, not a belly-itcher!" is being a bad sport. Even worse, and potentially dangerous, is shouting "Drop it!" to the fielder waiting under a fly ball. The goal of those doing the chattering is to mess with, and mess up, the other team's players.

Block out the noise and focus on what you're there to do. Noises in life, like those on baseball and softball fields, can make whatever you're trying to do harder. And there are so many noises: someone is always whispering, passing notes, or giggling in class; your phone has too many tempting games and posts; you get too many texts. How good you are at ignoring the chatter of life can be the difference between winning and losing, between getting something done right and not getting it done at all. When you're up to bat, it's just you and the pitcher; when you're pitching, it's just you and the catcher; when you're in the field, it's just you and the ball. Ignore everything else. Lock in and block out.

Taunting is a special type of noise—one that is mean and meant to hurt. Gossip is a real-life example of baseball and softball field taunts. There will always be those who feel better when they're embarrassing others. In baseball and softball, the best teams and the best players don't taunt. Speak with your actions and your successes, not with taunting. Gossiping may be entertaining, or make you feel that you're better than others, but it can cause real hurt and be dangerous. When others gossip about you, use it as a chance to toughen up. Believe in yourself, who you are, and what you can do, so you can ignore mean and untrue things people might say about you. People who gossip about you are trying to embarrass you or make you unhappy. Don't let them get to you. Block out the gossip. When they taunt "Hey batter, batter," what they really mean is, "Hey, I wish I was better."

11

Pitchers

Unexpected Changes
Family and Personal Crises

Hitting a baseball or fast-pitched softball is one of the toughest challenges in sports. If human pitchers were just a little more like those pitching machines in the batting cage, consistent in their speed and angle, it would be a whole lot easier to hit during a game. But human pitchers purposely change their pitches a lot; they try to fool the hitter by changing the speeds, spins, and locations: inside or outside, high or low, or right down the middle. Breaking balls mess up the timing of the batter expecting a fastball. A sidearm pitch confuses the hitter who's expecting one from over the top. A wild pitcher may cause a batter to change where they stand in the batter's box.

Life is not a pitching machine. What happens in life isn't always what we expect. Our plans get messed up; activities are canceled or added to our day; our focus is changed by what other people do or say. Instead of doing one thing, circumstances force us to do something else. Don't get upset or panic because of life's many spins and angles. Do the best you can when you're expecting a fastball, but if life throws you a curve, you may have to change how and where you stand in the batter's box to hit the pitch. Your first swing may be way off. Learn from it so the next swing is better. In baseball and softball, it's just a pitcher and it's just a ball. In life, a substitute teacher is still just a teacher. A new boss at your after-school job is still just a boss. Sleeping at camp or at a friend's house is just another bed and pillow. High school is like middle school, only with bigger kids, bigger hallways, and more homework. You may have to change where you stand in life's batter's boxes, but a new house is still a house, and a new town is still a town. They will soon feel comfortable and safe if you are patient and able to accept the change. You'll make new friends just like you made your old friends. The pitching machine can help you practice, but it's too easy to use all the time and it gets boring. Real pitches from the real pitchers in your real life can be more fun and interesting if you give them a chance.

Sometimes, though, life throws you a really bad curveball. Terrible changes, like your parents' divorce, a grandparent's death, or you getting sick, can take you completely out of the game. But even when a terrible thing happens, you have to try to deal with it the best you can. There is no easy way to handle awful things, but you have to try to stay in the batter's box, stay in the game. Your parents both love you even if you all won't be living together anymore. Try to see the change as giving you two happier, loving households. Get through a grandparent's passing by finding comfort in the wonderful memories you have. Although they won't be there with you tomorrow, they were there for many days before and you made them happy and proud. If you get sick, know that your family, friends, doctors, and nurses are all on your team, in the dugout with you—you are not fighting alone. There are people who love you and support you and will spend the time and energy to get you through even the toughest times. And if you can get through enormous challenges like these, everything else life throws at you in the future will feel more like a pitching machine and easier to handle.

12

The Count

Improve Your Chances for Success Handling Disappointments

In the one-on-one battle between pitcher and batter, the count—the number of balls and strikes—tells everyone who's winning and losing the battle. "Working the count" means batters are trying to get to a count that's better for them. That means knowing when to swing, when not to swing, and, if possible, fouling off good pitches to "stay alive" at the plate. When the batter is ahead in the count, the pitcher must throw a strike—usually the fastball right down the middle that the batter wants. When the pitcher is ahead, though, the batter can expect tricky changeups and curveballs, and pitches too high or too low to be hit well. When batters are ahead, they don't have to swing at a pitch unless they really like it. When pitchers are ahead, they can "waste" a pitch hoping the batter will swing anyway.

Life is full of counts. Sometimes you're leading in the count, other times you're trailing. You should "work the count" to improve your chances of winning each battle. Your count is good for getting "a hit" on a homework project due in a week if you plan your work to finish it on time. The count goes against you if you wait until the night before the assignment is due to start it. Same with a test. If you start studying a few days ahead of the test, you're ahead in the count. If you wait until the last night to study, the count goes against you, and you may strike out and fail the test. You never know what might come up at the last minute to stop you from studying the night before the test. Want your parents to give you a little extra time before lights out at night? If you help clean up the dinner dishes or straighten your room, your count improves and so do your chances of getting the bonus time for what you want to do. If you fight with your brother or sister, your count gets worse, and your parents are less likely to give you what you want. Don't let the count get to where you *must* swing to not strike out. Get ahead in the count, so every next pitch life throws you is a fastball right down the middle.

Sometimes you can't stop the count from going against you—bad calls by the umpire, sneaky pitches by the pitcher, or your own mistakes at the plate. A batter often faces disappointments. When you're "down in the count," change how you are hitting—choke up on the bat, shorten your swing, be less picky, and just try to put the bat on the ball to make something happen. Off the field, you also have to change what you're doing when the count goes against you. Ask your teacher for extra help in a class that's giving you trouble. If you lose the student council or club election, volunteer to help with activities anyway. If your friends are being mean to you or not including you, talk to them and ask them why. If they don't give you a good answer or don't change the way they act toward you, you unfortunately might have to find new friends. Not every swing in life results in a big hit and not every pitch is hittable. Disappointments happen. You may have to settle for worse results than you're hoping for until the count is better on your next at-bat.

13

The Called Strikeout

Take a Chance
Try Again

There are two kinds of strikeouts—swinging and called. Both are painful for batters, because they didn't put the ball in play. The called third strike, though, feels worse because it comes from standing there and doing nothing. Batters should do their best to *never* take a called third strike. When there are two strikes, no matter how many balls, the batter has to "protect the plate." Meaning the batter can't look for the perfect or even close-to-perfect pitch—if the pitch is close enough that the umpire *might* call it a strike, the batter has to take a chance and swing at it. That means with two strikes, the batter has to be *ready* to swing, *plan* to swing, and then *SWING* at the next pitch unless it is so far out of the strike zone that even *this* umpire will call it a ball.

There are times in life where another strike would be really bad news. At those times, take a chance you'll go down swinging, protect the plate, and swing. If you don't swing, you may go down anyway—but if you go for it, you just might get a hit. Protect the plate in class at school. It's better to take a chance and turn in a homework assignment you haven't quite finished, or you're not completely satisfied with, than to not turn it in at all. If your teacher offers a make-up test for a bad grade, take it. And even if you're not offered a makeup test, take a chance and ask for one—the teacher may say "No," but if you don't ask you'll never know. The homework or makeup test may not be perfect or may even turn out badly, but taking a chance is better than not swinging at all when you're down two strikes.

When you're down two strikes, learn from those earlier pitches and try again. Try out for the band, school play, or softball team again next year. Run for student council again at the next election. Reapply for the summer job you didn't get last year. The people who said "No" the first time, or even the second time, often reward those who stick with it and keep on swinging.

14

The Swinging Strikeout

Make Good Decisions
Right and Wrong

Strikeouts from swinging at bad pitches are almost (almost!) as bad as taking a called third strike. But it happens all the time. Nervous batters swing at everything the pitcher throws at them, hoping for a lucky hit or at least to be done with the at-bat. They swing at curveballs in the dirt, fastballs above their shoulders, pitches too far outside to reach. The only time batters should swing at a pitch they don't *love* is when there are two strikes and the next pitch could be close enough for the umpire to sit the player down with a called third strike. But until there are two strikes, the batter should be picky and patient. Just making contact with a pitch isn't good enough—the confident batter wants to hit the ball hard and far. To do that, the pitch must be one with which the batter can do some serious damage.

There is no reason to swing at bad pitches off the diamond, either. And there will be lots of them. Other kids doing things they shouldn't, dares you shouldn't take, parties you shouldn't go to, older kids offering car rides you should avoid, apps you shouldn't use—these are all pitches in the dirt you shouldn't swing at. Make good decisions and use common sense to not swing at the bad pitches.

Think carefully about each pitch others throw at you. Know the count, know what's right and what's wrong, know what you should and shouldn't do. You've been taught well by those who mean the best for you. Listen to their advice. It's rare in life to have no choice, to be down two strikes, where you *must* do something you know is wrong. The right option or opportunity will come if you're patient and confident. Wait for the right pitch, your pitch, the one you *love*, before taking a swing—and then hit it hard and far.

15

The Check Swing

Changing Your Mind
Admitting Your Mistakes
Keeping Your Promises

If batters start to swing, and then stop before their wrists go too far, the umpire should not call a swinging strike. Checking, or holding up, before finishing a swing lets batters get a head start on their swing but still gives them an escape. The check swing is used most by two types of hitters: those who "attack" pitches and hope to meet the ball well out in front of the plate, and those who struggle with whether to swing at all. It can be hard for umpires to tell if the check swing has gone too far, so they often call it a strike even though the batter tried to hold up.

Some pitches in life come at you fast and right down the middle. Others curve and are confusing. Even after you've started to do something, it's okay to change your mind if the pitch surprises you or veers way out of the strike zone. You may have started to do something or go somewhere you now realize you shouldn't have. If you haven't gone too far with it, you may still be able to change your mind. Your friends talk you into playing a prank on your teachers, but when you see it might hurt their feelings or be dangerous, back out and don't be a part of it. On a bike ride with friends, they challenge you to race them down the big hill but when you start down you realize it's too steep—lose that challenge and walk your bike down safely. You're ready to leap off the cliff and into the lake below when you realize you don't know where the rocks are—climb down the hill and go for a swim without the dive.

Understanding you've made a mistake in the middle of what you're doing shows you're thoughtful and able to consider what you're doing even while you're doing it. It also shows you're not afraid to dive in or, if necessary, back out. Admitting the mistake to yourself and to others may be embarrassing, but proves you're honest and humble enough to know you're not perfect.

Changing your mind *all* the time and with *every* pitch in life can make people think you have trouble making up your mind or keeping promises. Be as careful and thoughtful about your decisions as you can; most times, you shouldn't change your mind and back out once you've promised to do something. Keeping your promises proves people can depend on you and trust you. Check swings are often called strikes because it can be tough for those watching to know if you really went too far before trying to back out. The more you check your swing, the more likely you are to strike out with those depending on you.

16

Dropped Third Strike

Second Chances

When the catcher drops the ball after the third strike, the batter can run to first base if there isn't already a runner there, or if there are two outs. This gives the batter a chance to get on base and erase the out. To get the batter out, the catcher now must find the ball and throw it to first base before the runner gets there. Hitters often forget this second chance—they're used to accepting the strikeout and going back to the dugout. After the catcher drops the third strike, batters may have already given up and only realize they should be running when they hear everyone else on their team and in the bleachers yelling, "Run!!"

You should always try to get it right the first time—be prepared for the pitcher, make good decisions, work the count, don't strike out. But when things don't work out the first time and you get a second chance, grab it and run with it. Sometimes life teaches lessons "the easy way," with no harm done, no out called. The deadline is changed to later for a homework assignment you forgot to do. A test you weren't ready for is postponed. The allowance money you thought you lost turns up in the washing machine. Don't wait for everyone to yell, "Run!!"

Be happy and relieved when life gives you a second chance after a mistake. Learn from the mistake and try not to make it again. Help others get a second chance, too. There will be times when *you'll* be in the dugout screaming "Run!!" as a teammate or a friend forgets what to do or loses their way.

17

The Walk

The Easy Way Is Not Always the Best Way

Four balls during an at-bat earn the batter a free pass to first base. Many batters, though, hate walks because they would much rather hit the ball. Other batters go to the plate hoping for a walk because they don't have enough confidence to swing the bat. Some players swing at pitches they shouldn't because they really want to hit and not walk, while others don't swing at pitches they should because they hope the umpire will show mercy and call four balls.

The thought of a free trip to first base can hurt both those who want it and those who don't. When it's your turn at the plate, don't look for a walk. Handle each pitch as it comes; swing at the good ones, let the bad ones go. Sometimes you do get a free pass in life, an easy way out of a tough spot. A lucky break, a nice coincidence, a fluke, perfect timing. When that happens, be happy to take the free pass. But if you go to bat expecting or hoping for a walk, always looking for the easy way out, you're likely to strike out waiting. Good luck comes more often to those who are prepared.

18

Taking a Pitch

Competing

After a batter has walked or been hit by a pitch, the next batter up can be in a good place with the pitcher who could be upset and shaky because they just put a runner on base. Coaches will often tell the next batter to "take" (not swing at) the first pitch after a pitcher's mistake. If that pitch is a ball, the coach may again tell the batter not to swing, sending the pitcher a message the hitter is going to wait and see if the pitcher can still throw a strike. A couple of balls thrown to this batter after the previous batter got a free pass will further shake the pitcher and may lead to more walks and hit batters, and more baserunners and runs.

As unkind as it may seem, taking advantage of an opponent's mistakes or bad luck is the way the game is played. This is not a bad thing. Getting ahead of others who are trying to do the same thing as you can be helpful to get what you want in life. Your first plan should be to make the most of yourself, be the best you can be. But knowing whom you're competing against is also important. There is a difference between getting ahead of someone in a cruel way and getting ahead in a smart way. Not swinging at a pitch or two from pitchers in trouble forces them to perform without you having to cheat or be sneaky or mean. There's nothing wrong with winning against someone else as long as it's done fairly and honestly. When you're applying for a summer job that others are also applying for, learn everything you can about the place where you hope to work, dress nicely for the interview and if you know someone who works there, ask them to put in a good word for you. Preparing a science fair project for a chance to win an award? If you have access to a color copying machine or 3D printer, use it to stand out from the others. When there are other people competing for the same thing as you, someone has to win. It might as well be you.

19

The Sacrifice

Help Others Get Ahead

A bunt and a fly ball can both be sacrifices, which means batters make an out that moves runners up on the bases to help their team. Even though the sacrifice isn't nearly as exciting as a home run, or even a single up the middle that drives in a run, the ability to sacrifice is one of the most important skills a hitter can have. The sacrifice only works, of course, when there are less than two outs—otherwise, it's too late; another out will end the inning and be of no help to the team.

There are times when your success is measured by how well others do. Sometimes being generous and helping others may set you back, but you'll feel good about your sacrifice even though you may be out—out of the time you spent or out the money or stuff you generously gave away. Recognize how fortunate you are to have what you have and to live where you live, and be conscious of those in your community and elsewhere in the world who are so much less fortunate. But don't wait too long to sacrifice for others because, like when there are already two outs, your sacrifice may be too late to help.

20

The Bunt

Slow Down and Simplify

A bunt is what happens when batters turn completely toward the pitcher, tighten their stance, turn their bat horizontal, and push the ball into the infield, hoping to move up the baserunners or surprise the fielders and reach first base safely. It's a lot easier to judge balls and strikes when bunting than it is with a full swing. The bunter doesn't have to bother with the usual stepping and swinging that can make it harder to put the bat on the ball. Bunting can also be the best way to handle a tough pitcher; it is simpler to make contact with a fastball or a breaking ball when the bat is right out in front of you than it is to find those pitches with a full swing starting from behind your head.

Bunting gives you a few extra split seconds to focus on the pitch, see the ball and judge where it's going. Is it a ball or a strike, a curveball or a fastball? The speed and curves of life often get in the way of your making good choices. All of the stuff you have to do every day can be like a tough pitcher, making you lose your focus on the important things, making it harder to put the bat on the ball. At those times, get into a bunting position and give yourself a few extra seconds to find the ball. Slow down and make it simpler to focus on the important things. Ask your teacher for a little more time on the big homework assignment. Drop an activity taking up too much of your time. Put away the computer, your phone, or the game device and go to bed a little earlier to get some extra sleep. Make a simple list of the three most important things you need to do and attack them one at a time, putting everything else off for a little while. Put the bat right out in front of you, tighten your stance, stare straight at the pitcher, and get a better view of the pitches coming at you.

21

The Suicide Squeeze

When Someone Really Needs You

Not all bunts are the same; some are more important than others. In most bunting situations, the batter actually follows through on the bunt only if it's a good pitch, which improves their chances of putting down a good bunt. Sometimes, though, with a runner on third base and less than two outs, and the team really needing to score a run, the coach will signal the squeeze play, telling the batter to bunt *no matter what* pitch the pitcher throws. As the pitcher begins his motion to the plate, the runner at third base streaks toward home plate with no turning back. If the batter *does* successfully bunt, the chances of the runner scoring are great because of the head start they had, running as fast as they can before a fielder can pick up the ball and throw it home. But if the batter *can't* put the bunt down, the pitch beats the runner to the plate and the catcher simply tags out the runner.

You'll be asked for many favors in your life—even many sacrifices. Most of the time, you'll try your best to help, and usually you'll be able to. But not all calls for help are the same. There are times when you absolutely must make it work because the people you care about are really counting on you. At those times, you should feel the needs of others as if they are your own needs. It may be your brother or sister, your parents, grandparents, best friend, or your partner on the school project. How you act when someone is really counting on you says a lot about who you are. The pitches for help may be difficult ones; they may require you to change your schedule or temporarily turn down someone who has a less urgent need. But this is a squeeze play—you have to do everything in your power to put the bat on the ball and come through for those counting on you the most.

22

Fake Bunts

White Lies

Sometimes, coaches will signal their batters to stand in a bunting position, but to then pull back when the pitch is thrown and *not* bunt the ball—even if the pitch is a strike. When the batter takes the bunting position, a lot of things happen in the field. The infielders all yell "Bunt!!"; the first and third basemen charge toward the batter; the second baseman runs to cover first base; the shortstop runs to cover second base. And, most importantly, pitchers often lose their focus and throw a bad pitch. That's usually the reason for the fake bunt—to shake the pitcher. Fake bunts are sneaky and a little dishonest. Coaches often call for them with a 3-and-0 count because they don't want the batter to swing on that count no matter where the pitch is thrown. By throwing off the pitcher's rhythm with the bunting position, and by causing everyone in the field near the pitcher running around yelling "Bunt!!" in the middle of his delivery, the chances of the pitcher throwing ball four go way up.

White lies are life's fake bunts, sneaky and a little dishonest. People who tell white lies usually mean to protect someone's feelings, to hide bad news, to prevent a fight, or to make a tough day easier for someone, including the person telling the white lie. But instead, white lies often backfire, hurting others by causing false hope and disappointment, and losing their trust. When your mom asks, "How was your math test today?" you may say, "Okay," even though you may think you didn't do well, because that little white lie saves you from having to deal with a bad grade until later. When your dad asks, "Have you seen anyone take anything from the liquor cabinet?" and you answer "No," you may have protected your older sister from your parents' punishment for now. When your mom asks if kids at the party were doing things they shouldn't, you might say, "I didn't see anything bad," to protect your friends (or yourself!). But the math test usually makes its way home from school, or at least the report card does. Your sister and her friends are too young to drink and may be driving later. And kids who do bad things at parties will usually get caught when they do even worse things later. When you "fake bunt" with white lies in life, you may think you're doing the right thing for other people, and you may even get out of a tight spot yourself—but just as the fake bunt triggers reactions on the field, white lies trigger reactions that can be very serious.

23

Small Ball

One Step at a Time

"Small ball" is a game plan to use bunts, stolen bases, well-placed outs, and hit-and-run plays to create runs, rather than relying on big hits, the "long ball." Many a big, strong, home run hitting team has been brought down by crafty small-ballers. Repeating these small-ball actions over and over can cause fielders to overrun the ball, overthrow the bases and, in their rush to catch the streaking runners, lose track of who's covering where. Runners move up, runs score.

Not all big accomplishments in life are home runs. Taking it one step at a time, slowly but surely moving forward, will often get you where you need to go better and faster than by trying to get there all at once. The top home run hitters often also lead the league in striking out. While at certain times in life thinking like a home run hitter and swinging for the fences are good ways of getting it done, being patient and taking small and smart steps can often work best. The win may be less exciting, but it can be more satisfying—and your chances of striking out go way down.

24

Hit and Run

Punctuality

Most plays by the hitting team are done by one player—a batter hits or a baserunner steals. At other times, the baserunner reacts *after* seeing the batter's hit. But in the hit-and-run play, like the suicide squeeze, two or more players must act at *exactly* the same time for the play to work. At the moment the pitch is thrown, the baserunner bolts for the next base and the hitter swings at *that pitch*, whatever and wherever it is. In successful hit and run plays, batters get a hit and move runners farther than they otherwise could have gotten just by stealing. If the batter hits the ball on the ground but gets out, the head start by the runner lowers the chance of a double play. Even if the batter misses the ball completely, their swing alone makes it harder for the catcher to throw out the runner.

Punctuality means being where you need to be, or doing what you need to do, on time. The hit-and-run play only works if hitters are on time, swinging exactly when they are told to swing. If class starts at 7:45 a.m., you're late if you arrive at 7:55. That's like swinging two pitches *after* the hit and run play is called—it doesn't help you or your team. The runners who are already moving depend on you swinging on time. It's not fair to others to make them wait for you or to think their time is less valuable than yours. When you are always late, those who count on you will stop waiting and find others who can swing the bat on time.

25

Home Runs

Gratitude
Overcoming Hard Times

When batters crack a home run over the fence, they and their teammates in the dugout jump and shout with excitement. The hitter calmly cruises around the bases, enjoying the thrill and taking in the moment while heading for home plate. The runs that score are even cooler because of the *way* they score. For most players, home runs are rare; some players never hit them. A home run is a big event for a player who has never hit one before, an important step forward in the growth of a ballplayer. To hit a home run over the fence, players need to be strong and have a lot of batting practice. They must pick good pitches, see the ball well, time their swing, and hit the ball right on the sweet spot of the bat. Everything has to come together perfectly for the player, at one second in time, and in one big and bold swing. Although it happens very quickly, a home run comes after many hours, days, and sometimes years of teaching by coaches who know how to put everything together for the perfect swing.

There are many big steps in your life. Your first steps as a baby, first time riding a bike, first day of school, first night sleeping away from home, graduation. And there are many more firsts to come. Each of them is an important step in your growth as a person, and each step depends on many things coming together at the same time. As you take each big new step in your life, remember you have been lovingly guided there by people who know what it takes to hit one out of the park. As you round third base and head for home in every important next step of your life, look up in the stands and blow a thank-you kiss to those special people. Without them, you might never have left the dugout.

Not every home run swing is perfect and not every home run clears the fence. "Inside-the-park" home runs happen when batters hit one far enough into the outfield—or into a hard-to-reach corner of the outfield—that they can speed all the way around the bases before the fielders get the ball back home. The score is the same as when the ball leaves the park, but inside-the-park home run hitters have no time to calmly cruise around the bases or wave to the fans. They have to streak from base to base, running as fast as they can to beat the throw. You don't take every big step in your life exactly the way you planned. Sometimes, the teaching and advice you get aren't perfect, some people along the way haven't been as loving as you would have hoped, the swing doesn't come together the way it should, and you're not able to clear the fence and smoothly cruise home. To get where you want to go, you may have to run much harder, making your own path and teaching yourself. But when you hit your inside-the-park home run, you can still be very proud—you got past the hard times along your way and scored despite them.

26

Foul Balls

Near Misses

The first- and third-base lines show where a fair ball is on the baseball and softball fields; anything hit outside of those lines is a foul ball. A foul ball is a near miss—everything from a near-miss home run to a near-miss strikeout. For the smart batter, a foul ball teaches a lesson during an at-bat. Each foul ball helps prepare batters for the next pitch and can tell them what is right and what is wrong with their swing. Right-handed batters who foul to the right are swinging late; they're swinging too early if the foul goes left (a lefty batter is just the opposite—left is too late, right is too early). A foul ball straight back is a perfectly-timed swing, but the batter hit the ball on its lower half—a more level swing may drive the next pitch straight ahead. Each foul ball improves the chances for a good hit on the next pitch.

Every day you swing the bat at new pitches life at throws you. Some of your swings become perfect hits the first time; other swings are near misses, foul balls that could have turned out better. A near miss is not a reason to quit or get down on yourself. It's a way to learn, and a chance to make a better swing next time. Understand every question you missed on your math test before starting on the next lesson to avoid making the same mistakes on the next test. If someone else got the spot on the team that cut you, practice harder before the next tryout. Forgot to do something important today? Write yourself a note so you'll remember to do it tomorrow. Each time you "foul one off," learn from the near miss and correct your swing until you get the hit you want.

27

Bases Loaded (Part 1)

Dealing with Pressure
Sticking with What Works

Coming to bat with the bases loaded makes many batters nervous. Whatever the score and whoever is watching, loaded bases change the way a batter thinks and acts. Fans, teammates, and coaches are yelling "Ducks on the pond!" "They're juiced!" "A walk's a run!" "They're out there for you!" Will it be a big hit? A walk that brings in a run? Or will it be a disappointing out? While more baserunners mean a better chance for runs, they also mean more pressure on batters—which may hurt their chances for getting a hit.

When the pressure is higher, put it in perspective. If you're worried about the "hardest test in your hardest class" or the "biggest tryout of your life," remember to think, "so far." There will always be bigger mountains to climb than those today, and then today's mountains will just seem like little hills. Remember all the high-pressure times in your past and how they now seem like no big deal. You got past them and moved on. You'll get past the "hardest" and "biggest" moments again today.

If you think about each new "huge event" and "most important time" with the same calm and self-confidence that help you do well in the regular events and times of your life, the pressure of loaded bases will fade away. Imagine the bases empty, or picture a simple batting practice before the game, and just do what you usually do. Sticking with what has worked well for you in the past can also turn a high-pressure event off the field into just another event—like the ones in which you do well all the time. Step up to the "bases-loaded" times in your life as you step up to your "bases-empty" times—ready and believing in yourself—but without feeling like it's such a big deal. You can hit the ball no matter how many runners are on base; it's just another at-bat and you've done it so many times before.

28

Switch-Hitting

*Just Because You Can, Doesn't
Mean You Should*

A few players have the special ability to hit from both sides of the plate—right-handed and left-handed. This gives them more choices at-bat—they can hit righty against a left-handed pitcher and lefty against a right-handed pitcher. Hitting from the opposite side that the ball is coming from gives the batter a slightly earlier look at the ball as it comes out of the pitcher's hand, and a better chance of following the pitch before having to swing. But in reality, most switch-hitters actually hit better from one side—which means they are really more natural and comfortable as a righty or lefty, but they continue to switch back and forth depending on whether the pitcher is a righty or lefty because they can, and because it *might* help them better hit the pitcher. Batters and their coaches need to decide whether switching to the other side of the plate will improve the batter's chances or make them worse by taking them away from their most natural stance.

Just because you *can* do something, doesn't mean you *should*. In life, just like in baseball and softball, your skills are only useful if they lead to something better. Making a traveling team doesn't mean you'll be happy leaving your friends on your old team. Being able to stay up and cram the night before a test and pass doesn't mean you wouldn't do better—and feel less anxious—if you studied for a few nights before the test. Knowing you can make other kids laugh doesn't mean you should talk back to your teacher, no matter how funny what you'd like to say is. Because you've jumped your skateboard off the high curb twice, doesn't mean trying this time from the top of the rail on the stairs won't land you in an emergency room. Use your abilities wisely, deciding when and where to switch from what usually works best for you.

29

Hit By the Pitch

Courage
Bouncing Back

The hardest thing to watch in a baseball or softball game, for players, parents, fans, and coaches, is a player getting hit by the ball. When a batter is hit by the pitch, there are two players who can get hurt. The batter obviously feels pain and might be afraid when coming to bat again, but the pitcher can also feel hurt, guilty, and embarrassed for having caused the pain and for giving up a free pass to first base. Pitchers who have hit a batter with a pitch can lose their focus, which could result in more bad pitches, walks, balks, and even more hit batters. And it's not only batters who get hit by the ball. Funny bounces hit infielders in the face; outfielders lose the fly ball in the sun and get knocked on the head; runners are hit by thrown or even batted balls.

If you don't want to ever get hit by the ball, you can't play the game. For some people, that's a reasonable choice to make. In life, many fun and usually wonderful activities sometimes hurt a person, either their body or their feelings or both. Afraid of getting hurt, some people choose to stay on the sidelines. It takes courage to step back into the batter's box after you've been hit by a pitch. But you'll be happier and feel better about yourself if you are able to get back in the game—and the sooner the better, before your memory of the pain makes it worse than it really was. "Shake off" the sting, because the rest of life is too much fun to miss.

It also takes courage to step back on the mound and pitch again after you've hit a batter or hurt someone in other parts of your life. If you're the one who caused the pain, you can't quit, either. Do your best to make up for it—apologize, help out in whatever way you can, and promise to be more careful in the future. And then you need to bounce back and move on. Constantly thinking about your mistake, even when it has hurt others, makes you lose your focus and your self-confidence—which can cause more bad pitches and even more pain.

30

The Last Out (Part 1)

The Big Picture

Baseball and softball are team sports, and no one player alone can win or lose any game for their team. The heroic diving catch doesn't win the game without the other outs made in the field that day. The clutch hit isn't a game-winner without the other hits and runs that came before. An error doesn't lose a game—if the game wasn't as close as it was, the error wouldn't have mattered. And the game was as close as it was only because of other plays that didn't work out. There are twenty-seven batters or runners on the losing team who make outs in a nine-inning game; the last of those outs is just one of twenty-seven made by that team. But being the last player standing, and then falling, can make players feel like the weight of the team was all on their shoulders—that it's all their fault their team lost.

Many things in life are team efforts where no one person alone can make or break the result. Try to see the big picture, not just your part of it. Your part in a team effort isn't always as important as you or others might make it seem. Usually, you are only in the position to fail *last* because *others* failed earlier, or because the skills you have shown before made you the best person to try now. It isn't all on your shoulders. You stand on the shoulders of others and others stand on yours, so don't take all the blame for a loss. But you shouldn't take all the credit for a win, either—your big hit or diving catch was only one of many hits and catches in the big picture.

PART III

ON BASE

31

Running to First

Focus
Trust Others

Running to first base is not the same as running to those that follow. Runners to second and third base must stop right on the base or risk being tagged out by an alert fielder. But after stepping on first base, the runner can run straight past it towards rightfield. The run to first is one of the easiest parts of the game to understand. The goal is straight ahead, easy to see, with a bright white line running right to it. Hitters just have to get there as fast as possible, never slowing down to watch their hit or screeching to a halt on the base. Just run like the wind. Nevertheless, too few players do it the right way because hitters often want to see where their hit went. Did it make it through the infield? Did it take a tough hop? Did the fielder bobble it? When runners to first base turn their attention away from running, they slow down, causing outs that could have been hits if only they hadn't lost their focus.

Don't lose your focus or let your attention wander. That will slow you down. Concentrate on what you're doing. See your goal straight ahead of you, figure out what you need to do to get there, and go—straight through, until you have safely crossed the base. Your science fair project won't get finished if the TV is on in the same room. Texting while you're mowing the lawn will leave bald spots in the yard, and texting while riding your bike . . . well, you know what can happen. Focus on the immediate undertaking, avoid turning away, and get it done right. Then there will be time for TV, texting, and friends.

If the ground ball gets into the outfield, the base running plan for the hitter changes. Now they have to "round" first base rather than running straight through it and look to see if they can possibly advance to second base. How can runners know which plan to use— running straight through, or turning and looking towards second base—if they're not watching where the ball goes and can only see what's right in front of them? That's the job of the first-base coach. Coaches are the eyes of the runners, telling them to "run through" or to "turn and look." There are times in life to completely depend on yourself to make the right choices, and other times to trust others to help you. Parents, teachers, counselors, clergy, coaches, doctors, and nurses can all help you at the important turning points in your life. Know your own goals and go all out to achieve them, but also know when to trust the eyes and wisdom of the more experienced coaches in your life who can see the whole field.

32

Turn and Look

Look Ahead
Ambition

Although baseball and softball seem to move more slowly and leave more time for thinking than other sports, there *are* times in a game requiring quick decisions. After batters hit a single past the infield and are running to first base, their coach will yell, "Turn and look!" as the runner gets close to first. This means rather than "running straight through" first base, the player should "round" it and take a short turn toward second base while finding where the ball is in the outfield. Runners and their coaches now make a quick yet crucial decision about moving onto second base. Without the turn and look, the runner settles for a single and misses the chance to get the extra base.

Whenever you finish something important to you, be proud of what you've done, but don't spend too much time being proud. It's time to look toward the next goal. Usually, you have to pause before taking life's next base. But sometimes, by thinking ahead, being alert, and acting quickly, you can advance a base or two just by smartly—and carefully—checking out the field and looking for a chance to stretch one big step into two. Enjoy each step ahead you take in your life, but always turn and look, thinking about second base even as you're still rounding first.

Ambition is what separates the excellent from the average. When you've been picked to sing in the chorus, practice hard in hopes of getting a solo. Getting an after school job is great, but being named weekend manager is even better. Joining a club expands your circle of friends and exposes you to new ideas—but every club needs a president! Push yourself for that extra base.

33

Leading Off

Balance Risk and Reward

When hitters reach base, their next responsibility is to be smart baserunners. The lead is the step or two or three that the runner "cheats" off the base before the pitcher throws the next pitch. The lead may be the difference between getting safely to the next base and getting thrown out trying. But, along with the leadoff comes a tradeoff—the risk the pitcher or catcher will trap the runner off base for an out. Too big a lead and the chances of being caught for an out go up. Too small a lead and the chances of getting to the next base go down. There are ways runners can lower their chances of being picked off base—watch for clues in the pitcher's leg movement; stand an exact distance from the base to make sure a dive will get them back just in time; and never take their eyes off the ball, even after it's in the catcher's glove.

Life is all about weighing the chances of a bad ending against the chances of a good ending. That's called balancing risk and reward. Taking too big a risk can mean losing everything; taking too little risk may mean winning nothing. As a runner, you learn the tricks of taking a lead. You also have to learn the tricks of taking risks in life. The right balance of risk and reward will lower the chances of a bad ending without giving up your chances to move up. Think carefully about your choices; talk to others who have had to make the same kind of choices; make a list of good things that can happen and bad things that can happen with a choice you are considering. Stay close enough to your safe spot so you can still dive back. Sometimes, even if you're being careful and thoughtful, you'll still get picked off—it happens to everyone. The pitcher's move to the base may be quicker and trickier than you thought it would be and you're out. But even when you get picked off, you can learn a valuable lesson that helps you make the next tough decision that comes along.

34

Stealing

Dangerous Behavior

Brave and fast baserunners can try running from one base to the next as the pitcher starts to throw the ball to the plate. Catchers then try throwing out the runners before they successfully steal the base. Whether runners get away with a steal or get caught depends on how big a lead they take and how fast they run, but also on factors they can't control—the pitcher's delivery, where the pitch ends up, the catcher's throw, and whether the fielder can catch the throw and tag the runner. If all goes right for the runner this time, they will be safe at the next base—and more likely to try again next time. But the next try at stealing a base may have a less happy ending if all the factors involved don't work in their favor again.

Whether or not you get away with risky or dangerous behavior depends on many things which may not be under your control. Running across a busy street without a traffic light, snowboarding or biking without a helmet, shoplifting on a dare (real life stealing!). You may get away with it safely this time, but if you get caught next time or the time after, the results could be terrible. If you get away with something risky or dangerous you may want to try it again, but the more times you do unsafe things, the less chance you'll end up safe. On the baseball and softball fields, although stealing is dangerous because the runner may get called out, it is an important part of the game and the worst that can happen is an out. In real life, dangerous behavior can have much more serious outcomes.

35

Sliding

Stay Safe

Baseball and softball sell a lot of laundry detergent. At every base except first, a runner hoping to beat a throw and "get under" a tag slides into the base. Players slide by dropping to the ground from their running position and thrusting their feet to the base—while moving at nearly full speed! Well-done slides end with runners' feet exactly touching the base so they get there fast and beat the tag. Runners don't need to slide every time they move to another base, but they should for any play that might be close. With a lot to gain and nothing to lose, runners should slide if there's *any* chance it may help avoid an out.

Buckle your seat belt, double-check the traffic before crossing the street, proofread your writing project for mistakes, tie your shoes, check your tires before jumping on your bike, lock the door, review your answers one more time before turning in a test, set two alarm clocks on important mornings. And, yes, don't run with scissors. When there is *any chance* a simple step might help you stay safe, why not?

Head-first slides ("diving slides"), where your hand is reaching for the base rather than your feet, are a different story. You may like this style because you think it gets you to the base a split-second sooner than a feet-first slide; or because a dive in the same direction you're running seems easier than dropping to your bottom while moving; or just because flying forward looks cool. But hands don't wear cleats. Injuries from jammed, broken, and stepped-on fingers happen a lot with head-first slides. While a feet-first slide is a simple way to stay on the base and not be an easy out, a head-first slide is a bigger risk than the out you're trying to prevent. Choices you make in life sometimes mean comparing the risks of one choice to the risks of another choice. The risk of being teased by your friends compared to the risk of going along with something you know is wrong. The risk of failing a test compared to the risk of getting caught cheating. The risk of getting caught lying to your parents about something you shouldn't have done, compared to the risk of telling them the truth and getting a punishment (hint: usually telling the truth is more important to your parents than the thing you shouldn't have done, so the punishment won't be so bad). Even if it means getting thrown out at base, don't make the risky slide—you'll need your hands (and your head!) for the next game.

36

First and Third

Freebies
Scams

A special baserunning moment happens with runners "at the corners," first and third bases, when there are less than two outs. With runners on first and third, the runner from first can usually steal second base without the catcher even trying to throw them out, because a throw to second would allow the alert runner to score from third base. That means a free base for the runner at first. The runner on third has to be careful, though, because teams in the field have "fake throw" plays to trap them if they start for home because they think the catcher is throwing to second base. Smart runners at third will stay close to the base until they see the throw heading all the way to second base before breaking for the plate.

Sometimes life gives a free base for the alert player. Take it. Passing on a freebie isn't being generous; it's a sign of being asleep on the bases. Libraries offer the best freebies of all—books, e-books, music, movies, and more. Free concerts in the park, free student days at the museum, free shows at school, and free upgrades for your computer or phone are all chances to "steal a base" without risk.

Like the runner on third getting caught off base by a "fake throw" from a sneaky catcher, though, not everything that looks like a freebie is real. Check with your parents if you're not sure about something that looks like a freebie but could be a trick. There are people out there who will try to trap you with offers too good to be true. Your parents are the best people to help you know if a freebie is real or a scam. The biggest scams for kids are online—if you use email or text messages, or play online games or are on social media, you'll get lots of offers for "free things" that aren't real. Those kinds of fakes can be expensive and dangerous.

37

Fly Balls

Reflexes for Quick Decisions

Baserunners have important decisions to make when their teammate hits a ball in the air with less than two outs. A fly ball that's *caught* is a potential double play if runners don't quickly get back to their base; this is especially risky with a line drive, which is caught so quickly a runner has little time to react. On the other hand, a fly ball *dropped* may mean a runner has to immediately run to the next base before the fielder can throw the ball there for a force out. There are ways for runners to avoid getting thrown out on a fly ball catch and help their chances of moving up to the next base. Runners should always "freeze on a line drive" to the infield and, on a fly ball not hit deep enough for a tag-up play (see the next chapter), "go halfway" to the next base. By freezing, runners don't get far enough away from their base that they can't get back after the line drive is caught. By going halfway, runners watch how the outfielder plays the ball: if it's not caught, runners can move to the next base with a big head start, but if it is caught, they can get back to their base with enough time to beat the long throw from the outfield. Freezing, going halfway, and tagging up are reflexes, which means you do them without having to think about it.

With time to plan ahead, get advice, and find help, it's easier to make the right choices when a tough decision comes up in your life. But you don't always have time to fully think things through or get advice. When you have to think fast and act even faster, you can rely on the reflexes you have practiced ahead of time. "You can meet really cool people on this website." "Smoke this." "Drink that." "What are you afraid of? Everybody's doing it!" These are all fly balls and you're the runner. Have a reflex answer that lets you do the right thing, sounding sure of yourself, without having to plan ahead or even ask advice: "No, I'm not interested." "Sorry, not my thing." "Not today, go without me." "Can't, my parents would kill me." Those reflexes show you know what you're doing, you're not afraid to say it, and you know the difference between right and wrong.

38

Tagging Up

Pause and Control Your Anger

Bases are tiny safety zones. When a fly ball is hit to the outfield, a rookie baserunner's first thought might be to take off from their base and run like the wind to the next base because they're excited by the crack of the bat. But when a fly ball is caught with less than two outs, runners are only allowed to move to the next base if they *first* tag up, coming back to touch their own base. They decide whether to tag up by how far the ball flies. The deeper it goes, the easier it will be to tag up. If runners run without tagging up and the fly ball is caught, they can be thrown out for a double play.

There will be times in your life when something excites you or makes you angry. You'll feel like doing something right away, without thinking. That's when it's time to tag up. Go back to your base before you do anything too quickly that you might regret. Pause and think about it for a little while in a comfortable and safe place and let your excitement or your anger chill a little. This short pause may not change what you decide to do—but waiting for a few minutes, hours, or even days usually won't change what you are hoping will happen, either. And if you change your mind about what's best to do while you're on base, you avoid the double play of being sorry and embarrassed for what you might have said or done impulsively without taking the time to think it over.

39

Running with Two Outs

When There Is Nothing to Lose, Go for It

When there are already two outs, runners on base begin dashing as fast and as hard as they can for the next base at the crack of the bat. No need to tag up or think about it with two outs. No matter where their teammate's hit goes, and no matter what kind of a hit it is, the runners have nothing to lose by running. There's no double play whether the hit is a fly ball or a grounder. While there's nothing to lose by running, there is often a lot to gain. The quicker start by runners not waiting to see the hit means they may get farther or even score on a base hit. Force outs and fielder's choices are harder for the fielding team if runners have a head start, making it more likely everybody will be safe.

With nothing to lose, and even a slight chance at getting something you want, why not try? Go for it! If the worst that can happen is the inning ends with you running, the inning would have also ended had you stood still—why not run as fast and as hard as you can and see what happens? Run for student council. Enter the math or history competition. Send your favorite painting to an art contest. Ask for something you really want—you may get it! The worst thing that can happen is you don't get it, but, if you don't try, there's no chance. When you find yourself in one of life's no-lose situations, see it as a chance to win.

40

Bases Loaded (Part 2)

Respect Others
Set a Good Example

There's room for only one runner on each base. Runners must always be aware of, and respect, what the runners ahead of them are doing. This is especially true when the bases are loaded, because the chances for force outs and double plays are so great.

Whenever you have the opportunity, look ahead, not behind. But if you move ahead too fast, without respecting others in your path, you may run right into a double play. No matter how fast or how smart you think you are, you can always learn from the steps and mistakes of those ahead of you. Your parents, grandparents, teachers, coaches, and older siblings have all been on this path before you, and their experiences and wisdom can help smooth your way. Running on your own, without looking ahead for advice and guidance, will hurt your chances to move up, and can get you in a pickle or even thrown out.

When it's *your* turn to be the lead runner, remember others are following and depending on your wise decisions. If you act too quickly without thinking, or you act too slowly because you're spending *too much* time thinking, you may hurt others' chances of moving ahead, and you're setting a bad example. Share the good decisions and good behavior you learned from others with those looking ahead at you and learning by your example. Kids in lower grades in school and, especially, your younger siblings are watching you and learning from you. Don't take their respect lightly.

41

Hidden Ball Tricks

Unhappy Surprises and Expecting the Unexpected

Trick plays don't happen very often in baseball, but the hidden ball trick, while rare, is beloved by players and fans alike. With a runner on base, the infielder closest to the runner's base will go to the mound to "talk" with the pitcher. There, the infielder will secretly take the baseball, hidden in the glove, back to their position. The pitcher steps on the mound, the runner takes their lead, and the sneaky infielder runs over and tags the runner out with the hidden baseball. Another trick gets played with a runner on second base. The pitcher fakes a pickoff throw to the shortstop, covering second base, who dives and pretends the ball has been overthrown into center field. When the runner "buys" the fake, they take off for third base and the pitcher tags or throws them out. To not get fooled by these tricks, runners should not take their lead from any base until they see the ball in the pitcher's hand, and not break for third base until they see the ball thrown past second and into the outfield.

Life is always playing tricks on you. Your plans may be ruined by unhappy surprises. Your cell phone dies and your alarm doesn't go off. Your bike gets a flat tire. Your computer crashes. Traffic makes you late. The dog eats your homework (really!). Sometimes you can avoid life's dirty little tricks by carefully watching the ball; expect the unexpected and have a backup plan in place. Charge your phone, back up your computer files, leave early in case there's traffic, tuck your homework in your backpack (and put your backpack up high where the dog can't reach it!). But many times, life's tricks catch you off base and there's nothing you can do about it. Things are not always under your control and life's surprises can get in the way of your best plans. When you get tagged out, what's most important is you learn from it. Try not to fall for the same trick again.

42

The Last Out (Part 2)

You Can't Do It All Yourself
Focus on the Real Goal

When a team is behind and up for its final at-bat, it really needs baserunners. If it's losing by only one run, the first runner to reach base safely is the potential tying run. Sometimes, in this situation, you'll take chances to try to tie the game: trying to stretch a single into a double, taking a big lead or stealing a base to get into scoring position. But when you're behind by *more* than one run, although the first runner to reach base is still important, more runners are needed to reach the real goal—winning the game. If the first runner doesn't see the real goal and tries to stretch a single into a double, or takes too big a lead, or tries to steal a base, they risk making a big out before their team has a chance to put the other runners they need on base. One runner trying to do too much can lose the game for the team.

When you face a challenge or a problem, you may feel like doing it all at once and doing it all yourself. But you often need the help of others to get important things done. To care for a pet, plant a backyard garden, run a lemonade stand, finish group projects at school, plan after-school activities, organize club programs, do volunteer work, or other big plans, you may need a team. Control your feelings of wanting to do it all yourself so you don't risk losing the game. Your part in how it all turns out is important but may not be the *only* or *most* important part of the real goal. Don't make the last out by trying too hard or taking on too much yourself.

Although a double looks better than a single on your personal stats sheet, getting thrown out to end the game while trying for that extra base only helps the other team. In a team project, focus on the real goal rather than on your own glory. When you try to do it all or be a hero to get more credit or be more popular, you put your whole team at risk of losing.

43

The Pickle

Pay Attention
Tell the Truth

The pickle, when a player is caught in a rundown between two bases, is one of the most exciting plays in baseball and softball. Fielders line up at each end and throw the ball back and forth, chasing the trapped runner, hoping to tag them out before they safely reach either of the two bases. How do runners get in this pickle in the first place? Usually by not paying attention and losing focus, getting surprised in their lead by a pitcher's pickoff move, overrunning a base, or trying to stretch a hit too far.

The best way to stay out of a pickle is not to get in one. True, sometimes it works out for the best and you either get back safely to where you started or even move up to the next base. But the stress you'll feel while in the middle—to say nothing of the chances of being tagged out—are too high a price for the small chance of gaining a base. Pickles in real life also often result from not paying attention. Daydreaming, thinking too much about the past, or looking too far into the future makes you miss life's signs and chances for moving up.

Stay in the moment, focus on what's going on right now, and don't get caught between bases.

One of life's most painful and upsetting pickles comes from lying. Getting caught in a lie puts you in a rundown between your parents, your teachers, your coaches, your friends. Sometimes you'll escape and get away with it. Most times you'll be tagged out. Every time you lie, you'll worry about getting caught. Even worse, you lose the trust of those around you. Everyone who catches you in a lie thinks you may be lying the next time too, putting you in a rundown even when you're safely standing on base and telling the truth.

PART IV

IN THE FIELD

44

The Ready Position

Good Study and Work Habits

The ready position is the way fielders stand as their pitcher prepares to throw the next pitch: legs slightly spread, arms out in front, and gloves open and waiting for the hit that may come their way. As fielders set up in the ready position, they show they are awake, aware, and alert—their bodies and their minds are both ready for anything that might happen next. They block out all the noise, look straight at the pitcher and the batter and are ready to spring into action.

Looking ready leads to *being* ready. Even if you are the most warmed-up player on the field and haven't missed any of your practices, you should make it a habit to snap into the ready position before every pitch. The ready position focuses your mind and your body on what's right ahead of you. In life off the diamond, the ready position also leads to good habits. Be awake, aware, and alert in class. Clear your desk before starting your homework. Make sure you have enough light before sitting down to read. Turn off your phone, the TV, and the loud music when you prepare for a test. The ready position leads to good study habits, good work habits, and fewer errors when handling the ball.

45

Around the Horn

Motivate Others
Share the Credit and Thank
Those Who Helped

One of the most curious baseball and softball traditions happens after a pitcher throws a strikeout, or an infielder makes an out. When there are less than two outs and no runners on base, the infielders proudly throw the ball to each other before the next batter steps to the plate. That's called throwing the ball "around the horn." The catcher or the first baseman usually starts it because one of them is holding the ball at the time of the out. The first throw is to the third baseman, who then tosses it to another infielder, who fires it to another, and finally back to the pitcher to face the next batter. Throwing the ball "around the horn" does two things for the fielding team. The first is to send "Congratulations!" to themselves and brag just a bit. "We just made an out! We're really good! We're really tough! The other team better watch out because we plan on doing it again!" The second, more important thing that happens with throwing the ball around the horn is giving a "pep talk" to motivate those infielders who were *not* part of making the out, sharing the credit, reminding them they are still very important parts of the game, and they have to be ready for action as the next batter steps up to the plate.

You rarely get great things done all by yourself. You need teamwork from those around you who give you support, cheer you on, and sacrifice for you. And, likewise, their ability to do good things depends on you. When you do well, remember to thank and praise those who helped; toss them the ball and tell them you couldn't have done it without them. Even if those in your group didn't help this time, you might not have been able to do what you did without their support in the past. By sharing the credit with others, you give your teammates a "pep talk," motivating them to do even better things for themselves and for you next time.

It's not just the infielders who help the team do well and deserve your thanks and cheers. When outfielders make a good catch, and especially when they make a *great* catch, the pitcher runs out toward them at the end of the inning, meeting them halfway to the dugout, to thank them for their outstanding effort. Pitchers know without the support of their great outfielders, flyouts would become hits and hits would become runs. No matter how far away or spread out your support group might be, give them a grateful high five when you do something big. Grandparents in another city, teachers from your former school, friends from your old neighborhood—even though they are far away in the outfield, they may have had big parts to play in getting you out of tough innings and they deserve your thanks.

46

The Shift

Your Reputation
Learn from the Past

Somehow, just nine players have to cover a huge baseball or softball field, so smart planning and positioning of each fielder is crucial for making outs. The usual positions for the fielding team are "straightaway," meaning the center fielder lines up behind second base; the right fielder is behind the second baseman, who in turn is between first and second base; and the left fielder is positioned behind the shortstop, who is between second and third base. The first and third basemen stand a few steps inside their foul lines and a few steps behind their bases. These are the positions fielders take when *nothing* is known about the batter. But when the fielding team has a history for the batters, when it knows their tendency to hit to one spot or another, it may *shift* its players' positions to predict where the batter is most likely to hit the ball.

History is the greatest teacher of all, and it tends to repeat itself. Your growth as a person is based on knowing and learning from your own history and from the past experiences of others. If certain ways you've acted, or things you've said, or people you've been with have gotten you where you want to go—and others have gotten you or people you know in trouble—shift what you do, what you say, and who you hang out with to take you in the right direction. Don't invite trouble by putting yourself in the wrong position and not learning from the past. Knowing where the ball has gone before should guide you in making decisions; in most cases, the shift you make will put you where you need to be.

Your reputation is what people who are important to you think about you, and it's one of the most valuable things you own. Your reputation affects how people treat you and whether they respect you. When people know you as someone who is honest and can be trusted, they will shift their treatment of you to show their trust. When in the past you've shown up on time, done what you've promised to do, and treated others nicely, most people will believe you will be that way in the future, too. A good reputation will last a long time, but the same is true of a bad reputation. Lying, not doing what you promised to do, not caring about others, and being lazy are labels which also will last a long time. When you have a bad reputation, people will also shift the positions they take towards you and, when that happens, it's very hard to change their minds about you.

47

The Grounder

Little Details Make a Big Difference

Baseballs and softballs take funny bounces, sometimes ferocious, sometimes atrocious. What starts out looking like a "routine" grounder may be the toughest play on the field. To play what looks like a routine grounder, infielders center their legs around the fast-approaching ball and keep their glove right between their legs, low to the ground to stop the ball from squirting under their glove and into the outfield. But even if the ball doesn't land right in the glove, and instead it takes a funny hop off fielders' arms or chests, they may still be able to make the play if they can keep the ball in front of them.

Problems happen when you let things slip. Routine plays in life, little details like places you must be and tasks you must do, get past you when you don't take them seriously or focus enough on them. Games are lost when the ball squirts under your glove. Getting done what you must do depends on paying attention to life's little details. Center yourself around the jobs you have to do. Keep a list and keep a calendar; take notes so you don't forget important things people have told you; respond quickly when someone is trying to contact you. Keep the ball in front of you—right in front of you where it's easy to see and remember how important the little details are. That way, even if surprise bounces happen—your schedule changes, a new assignment comes up, a friend needs your help right away—you can still make the play.

48

The Pop Fly

Take Charge
Keep Your Promises
Follow Through

The pop fly is the scariest play in baseball and softball—at least for the fans watching in the stands. The pop fly gives players time to run to the ball and camp under it. In fact, the ball is in the air for so much time, something bad can happen—and often does! Too many fielders can get there at the same time, each looking straight up, gloves ready, followed by them all crashing into each other and the ball dropping to the ground between them. Or, all the fielders yell, "Mine, mine, mine" as they gather under the pop fly, only to politely back away as the ball falls back to earth, followed by the upset players pointing fingers at each other.

Take charge. There are tasks in life which more than one person might be able to handle and it's not clear who should be doing it. Someone must step up, call the ball, and wave everyone else off so there won't be a crash. One voice has to be louder. When you're in the best position to lead a project, settle a tough situation between friends, or speak for a cause, call the ball.

Keep your promises. Once you've said you'll take care of it and you're in charge, do everything you can to do what you've said you will. When people are relying on you because you've committed to something, don't let them down. And then be ready and willing to take credit for the good catch, or to accept blame for the miss.

Double-check everything you do with others to make sure you know who is doing what. If you're the one "calling" for the ball, make sure others hear you; if someone else is calling for it, make sure you hear them. Messages you send can get lost and so can messages people send to you. When it's important your message—or assignment or project—gets where it's going and gets seen or heard, follow through and make sure it got there. Otherwise, you've dropped the ball.

49

Shortstop and Right Field

*Make the Most of Every Chance
Beat Expectations*

Many think the best fielder on the team plays shortstop, and the worst plays right field. Shortstop is the "star" position every good player wants to play. Right field is seen as the best place, besides the bench, to hide less talented players so their playing won't hurt the team. But in many games, as many or even more balls go to the right side of the field, second base and right field, than to shortstop. The better and faster the pitcher, the later right-handed batters will swing, and the greater the chance that hits will go to right field. And left-handed batters will often "pull" the ball to right fielders when facing slower pitchers. Right field can be a busy place!

Make the most of every chance you get. If you're put in to play right field, see it as a chance to prove yourself rather than seeing it as an insult. The chances of a ball coming to you are greater than you or the coaches may expect—be ready to surprise everyone with how well you play. If you're assigned to the chorus instead of getting a solo, or you're a writer for the school paper instead of the editor, or one of the color guard team instead of the captain, be the best chorus singer, writer, or color guard you can be. Become an expert at whatever you're asked to do.

You won't always get your first-choice position, but whatever you're given, you'll have the chance to make a great play and beat expectations. Making the play no one expects you to make can be much bigger than making the play, as a shortstop for example, that everyone does expect. Because people expect less of rightfielders, they face less pressure than the shortstop (and any other position on the field!). The less people expect of you, the better your chance to impress.

50

First Step In, First Step Back

First Impressions
Get Off to the Right Start

When the ball is hit, fielders react fast. On a soft ground ball, infielders don't wait for the ball to come to them; instead, they "charge" the ball, taking their first step *in* and moving straight to the ball. This gives the infielder a chance to grab the ball on a better bounce and make a quicker throw to first base. But when a fly ball is hit to the outfield, outfielders take their first step *back* because moving backward is harder than moving forward; it's easier to correct a wrong first step back by running forward than it is to fix a wrong first step forward by running back. The right first step gives fielders their best chance of making the play.

First impressions are your first steps in new relationships—with teachers, coaches, bosses, friends, and others. Make the right first impression, and you're off to a good start. But the wrong first impression is hard to correct and may send you running backwards to chase a ball that's gotten past you.

Get off to the right start on every play. Before starting a new assignment, project, test, or job, your first step should be to decide how hard it is and how long it's going to take so you can pace yourself. On your first day in a new school, get there early to scout out the important places—bathrooms, cafeteria, gym, auditorium—so you feel comfortable. Arriving early for your first day at a summer job creates the right first impression and sets the tone with your boss and co-workers for the rest of the summer. When someone asks you to do something you're not sure is right, take a step back and say, "I'll need some time to think about that." But if an opportunity comes up that you know is right for you, charge the ball and grab it before it gets away from you. The right first steps give you a better look at where the ball is going and a little more time to judge the bounce before making the play.

51

The Stretch at First

When to Reach Out
When to Pull Back

One of the reasons first basemen are picked to play that position is their ability to "stretch." Throws from the infield to first base can be long, off-balance, and off target. First basemen must catch the ball while keeping their foot on the base to get the out. Talented first basemen can stretch toward the ball like a rubber band without taking their foot off the base. But they also have to judge when they won't be able to make the stretch. If the throw is too far off target, first basemen must leave the base and catch the ball wherever it flies. If the ball gets away from them, the runner not only reaches first base safely, but may even advance to second base.

To "stretch" off the field, you don't need to have a certain body type; you only need to have an open mind. Join a new club or try a new sport. Be part of a group doing good work in your school or community. Even if it's difficult, reach out to support a friend who needs your help. Not everyone can or will make these stretches, but if you do, the rewards are great; those you've helped will be grateful, those who saw what you did will know the kind of person you are, and you will feel great for the good you've done.

You must also realize when a stretch is too far and may be a bad thing to do. Those are the times when, like the first baseman, you need to pull your foot off the base and not stretch further. Friends or classmates in trouble may ask you to cover up or do dangerous things for them. Even if you mean well and would like to help a friend, those are stretches that go too far. Know when to reach out to help, but also know when to pull your foot off the base so the ball doesn't get past you and make things worse.

52

The Double Play

Patience

A double play happens when two outs are made on the same play. Double plays can change the whole game, shutting down a rally by the hitting team and exciting the players on the fielding team. The two most common types of double play are a fly ball that is caught with a baserunner trapped off their base and a ground ball to the infield that is quickly picked up and thrown from one base to another, getting two runners out. The first type is common; the second is harder and doesn't happen very often in youth games—and trying it can cause errors. When fielders are rushing to turn the double play, they may bobble the ground ball or throw the ball wildly so it ends up in the outfield or in the bleachers.

There's a time for everything. Don't try to make *too* much of every chance in life. Patience can prevent a bad error. You must walk your dog *and* bike to the store—having Fido run behind your bike may hurt him and get you in an accident. Doing your homework on the bench in the dugout at your game may make you miss exciting moments for your team or your coach's instructions, and you may mess up on your homework. Texting your friends while skateboarding to the park—terrible idea! If the perfect chance for the double play comes your way, a chance to successfully accomplish two things at once, go for it, but realize one out is better than none. If you try to do too much before you're ready, you may bobble something and put yourself in a worse position. With more than one task to accomplish, be patient. Sometimes it's better to hold onto the ball than to throw it away, especially when the chances for that second out are low. The ball in the hand is better than the ball in the bushes.

53

Fielder's Choice

Deciding What's Most Important
Homework and Tests

With runners on base, infielders must decide where to throw the ball after they field a ground ball. With less than two outs, the most important thing is to get out the "lead" runner, the runner closest to reaching home and scoring. For example, with a runner on first base, the fielder will handle the grounder and throw the ball to second base to force out the runner coming over from first. Sometimes, like when the first baseman, pitcher, or catcher fields the ball, the throw to second base is longer and harder to make than just tossing to first base, but the reward is the fielding team has now made an out without allowing the opponent to move closer to home. If there are already two outs, the most important thing for fielders is to "get the easy out," meaning throw the ball to the closest base. When you're in the field and there are runners on base, plan ahead for what you'll do if the ball comes to you. Picture the play you'll make so you know where to throw the ball.

Decide what's most important for the whole game and for each choice you must make in life. Sometimes, like when there are two outs and runners on base, do whatever's easiest and safest to get the job done. Get the easy out and move on to the next inning. But sometimes you must make the longer throw and the tougher play. Showing up for a neighborhood event you're not excited about is polite and doesn't take much effort—just being there for a little while will be enough. But when a family member or close friend needs your help in a tough situation, that's the time to make the long throw and give your best effort, however difficult it may be.

Decide what's most important in school. With a lot of homework assignments, finish the ones due tomorrow first, even if others are more interesting or fun. When you have tests, choosing the easiest and safest path—studying for the tests on the subjects you like best—might let runners move up and hurt your grades for the whole year. That's when you make the harder, longer throw, studying harder and longer for the toughest tests in the "boring" subjects—because what's important is not only getting the job done, but also the bigger picture, the whole game. The night before each test, study just for that test so it's fresh in your mind, but use the time *before* that night to study ahead for the tests you're most worried about. Decide what's most important and plan ahead so you'll make the right choice when the ball gets to you.

54

Bases Loaded (Part 3)

Plan Ahead
Ask for Advice

Fielders have many choices if the ball comes to them with bases loaded. Sometimes, it feels like too many choices. With all those decisions to make, with so little time to make them, and with all those runners moving with the crack of the bat, fielders may panic if the ball comes to them. They may blow the play, or field the ball perfectly but then be confused about what to do next and freeze long enough so that everyone is safe everywhere. More than any other situation in baseball and softball, when the bases are loaded, fielders must plan ahead. They must imagine the play happening *before the pitch is thrown*, planning exactly what they'll do if a ground ball, a line drive, or a pop-up comes their way.

Life can be complicated, with lots of choices to make. When the bases are loaded, you need to plan ahead and imagine what you're going to do *before* tough decisions come up. Friends hanging with the wrong crowd or doing the wrong things. Bullying by the school jerk. Classmates asking to copy your homework or test. People you don't know reaching out to you on social media. What should you do in those situations? When those sorts of choices come up in your life, the bases are loaded and the ball is heading your way. If you haven't pictured the play you're going to make before it happens, you might blow it.

When you're feeling like you might panic because there are too many things moving all at once, your smartest play is to find someone to advise you. Your parents are the best choice, but there are others who can help—your older sibling, the school counselor, a favorite teacher, your clergy. Those you confide in will be happy you trusted them to help you and be proud of you for planning ahead, not panicking, and making the right play.

55

Cutoffs and Relays

Get Help

When the ball is hit to the outfield with runners on base, the *infielders* jump into action, too. The throw from the outfield to the infield is long and the baserunners are moving fast. To help the outfielder get the ball to the right place and try to stop the runners from going too far on the bases, an infielder will dash part way into the outfield to become the "cutoff," get the throw from the outfielder and relay it to the right place. Rather than trying to figure out where all the runners are, where the ball is supposed to go, and then throwing it there themselves (all in the few seconds after fielding the ball), outfielders can focus on fielding the ball and then just "hit the cutoff" who is standing right where the outfielder expects them to be. Outfielders trust their cutoffs to do the right thing with the ball. There's a lot going on all at once, but the cutoff simplifies the situation for the outfielders. Outfielders who "miss" their cutoff teammate may make a bad throw to the wrong place and let runs score.

For the tough jobs, hit your cutoff teammate. When there's too much going on in your life, focus on the most important thing and get help for everything else. Getting help doesn't mean you're weak or lazy. Instead, it shows you understand how much there is to do and how important it is to get it done and get it done right. Speak to your parents or teacher about getting a tutor. Ask if a coach might be able to work with you on a weekend instead of a school night. Most importantly, if you are feeling too much stress from everything you have to do or from the pressure people are putting on you, ask your parents or your school for a counselor to help you talk about it. There are ways for dealing with every problem and all the troubles you may face in your life—but you must know yourself well enough to know when to get help, when to "hit your cutoff"—people you trust to help you—so the ball ends up where it's supposed to go.

56

The Warning Track

Listen to Warnings

At the edge of the outfield, the grass ends at a thin strip of dirt that runs along the edge of the fence. This warning track reminds outfielders who are worried about chasing and catching a fly ball, with their eyes turned up to the sky, that the wall is coming up fast. When fielders' cleats hit the dirt patch, they know to slow down or stop running backwards so they don't crash into the fence. Thanks to the warning track, the ball may hit off the wall, but the player won't.

Warnings protect you from crashing. When you are too worried about something, you may not see the risks or dangers coming up fast. You may have worries about whether you're popular, what your friends think about you, and what you need to do to keep those friends. You may be thinking about what you're missing by "wasting" your time studying and sitting in class. You may get bad advice from your friends about how to get around the rules at school or at home. Those kinds of fly balls can get you running backwards with your eyes to the sky, and make you forget you're coming dangerously close to hitting the wall. When you get a warning from your parents, your teachers, your coaches, or a kind school safety officer, hear it and obey it. Feel your cleats hit the dirt so you don't crash.

57

Errors

Grow from Your Mistakes
Stay in the Moment

There are three types of errors—fielding, throwing, and mental. Fielding and throwing are skills that can be practiced and improved but will never be perfect. Mental errors are those that happen when you aren't thinking clearly. Examples of those kinds of errors are throwing the ball to the wrong place, running at the wrong time, taking too big a lead, swinging at a bad pitch, or missing a coach's sign. Errors frequently pile up on top of each other. A fielding error may lead to a rushed and bad throw. One bad throw can lead to another as runners keep running and fielders keep trying to catch them. Once fielders bobble a grounder, they may be so desperate not to make another mistake that mental errors creep in. Focusing on the last play can lead to wrong decisions on the next one. Errors made by fielding or throwing are counted and scored in the scorebook because they end up with a runner gaining ground due to the mistake. But even though mental errors never get into the scorebook, they are the most embarrassing of all and can change the way a play or the whole game ends up.

People are not perfect, and they make mistakes. One way to measure yourself as a player—in baseball or softball, and in life—is what you do, and how you do it, *after* you make an error. Do you hang your head, kick the dirt, throw your helmet, and lose your focus? Or do you pound your glove with your fist and move on to the next play? Do you lose your confidence and let the errors pile up, or do you tell yourself it was just one play, one mistake, one more chance to learn? Do you make excuses and blame others, or do you take extra practice to work on the type of play that went wrong? Errors may lead to runs scored, games blown, even championships lost. But tomorrow, the sun rises, and another game begins. Errors are lessons learned the hard way, but also chances to grow before the next day and before the next play.

Keep focused to prevent mental errors. When you're on the field, the only game that matters is this game, and the only part of this game that matters is the part going on right now. Losing your focus comes from thinking about yesterday's game or a play from the last inning. It comes from worrying about tomorrow's problems or what you have to do next week. At important times in your day, block out the past and the future and lock into this one moment. Lock into this play, this pitch, this tryout, this homework assignment, this test. Be completely "in" the here and now, in the moment, in *this* moment. Focus on what you're doing until it's finished, and then it's okay to think a bit about yesterday and tomorrow.

58

Back-Ups

Acts of Loving Kindness

No sports pay more attention to what can go wrong than baseball and softball. For most balls hit or thrown on the field, it's clear which fielder should be making the play. But as soon as the ball is on the move from the bat or a throw, at least one and sometimes two other fielders are also on the move to "back up" the play. They get close behind the main fielder on that play in case the ball gets past. The ball hit or thrown to third base gets both the shortstop and the left fielder running behind the third baseman to back up the play. The center fielder backs up hits to second base and right or left field. The catcher backs up some throws to first base or third base, and the pitcher backs up throws to the infield and to home plate.

As a fielder, knowing teammates "have your back" lets you feel less anxious, because if you make an error, an alert back-up play can save the day. And often it's not your error causing the ball to get past you—bad hops are part of the game. Just as you feel better knowing someone is behind you, you should be there to back up others. Nine players stand ready for action on baseball and softball fields, each supporting the others. In the larger teams in your life, you also must support others, and they must support you. Giving to and collecting for charity, feeding the hungry, helping to find or build homes for those experiencing homelessness, lending a hand to the disabled and elderly, volunteering at the pet shelter, defending those whom others pick on, and so many other acts of loving kindness are ways for good teammates in the world off the diamond to give back-up and stop the ball from getting past. Bad hops are part of the game of life, too.

PART V

ON THE MOUND

59

The Mound

Stand Up for What You Believe
Pick Your Battles Carefully

Rising from the center of the otherwise flat infield, the mound is the "stage" for pitchers where they deliver their best stuff. This pile of dirt gives pitchers an advantage, letting them throw downhill. From the mound, their fastball has more force and speed, and their curveball has more room to curve.

When you feel strongly about something important, stand up for what you believe. It may be easier to avoid attention and shrink away from tough positions—which is okay if it's not that important to you. But when it really matters, don't slink away with the others to flat ground where your voice is harder to hear. Climb up on the mound, take center stage. Be a leader in speaking up for what you strongly believe. Support others who feel the same way and may not be as bold to take the lead. Find a "high ground" to deliver your best stuff; send your message loud and clear, with force, and stay strong. Know what you stand for and stand tall for it.

Your mound should be saved for the times you really need it. If you take a strong stand for *every* opinion or idea you have or *every* time you disagree with someone, people won't take you seriously when something comes up that is truly important to you. Pick your battles carefully. Don't risk being seen as a nag or a pest. Then when you step up and fire your best stuff, people will listen.

60

Lefties and Righties

Stereotyping

Whether you're right-handed or left-handed is a big deal in baseball. Left-handed pitchers are brought into the game sometimes just to pitch to left-handed batters. Switch-hitters bat lefty against a right-handed pitcher and righty against a lefty pitcher. Lefty throwers play first base and outfield, but usually don't play catcher, second base, shortstop, or third base because the turns and angles of those positions come far easier for righty throwers. Righties, on the other hand, can play all positions, but a lefty might beat out a righty to play first base just by being a lefty. Really, though, the labels "righty" and "lefty" can lead to the wrong idea about someone. While the differences between righties and lefties may be real much of the time, they are not true *all* the time. On any day, and in any game, any lefty pitcher may strike out a right-handed batter—or not. A right-handed fielder may be much better at first base than a lefty—or not. A lot depends on the player, not just whether they're a righty or lefty.

Stereotyping means treating someone differently because of the label you or others have given them. Stereotyping leads to treating people unfairly, and to missed chances to play certain positions in baseball, softball, and in life. When how you feel about people and what you expect of them is based on whether they are a righty or lefty—or on their skin color, their religion, whether they are a boy or a girl, tall or short, thin or heavy, rich or poor—you are taking away their right to be seen and judged as a person, an individual, rather than as a member of a group. It's not all about whether someone is a righty or lefty, it's about what kind of player they are, who they are as a person, not as a label. When you assume things about people without getting to know them, you're usually wrong.

61

Rituals

Good Routines

Baseball and softball are rich in rituals. Rituals are actions you do over and over for good luck or because they make you feel more comfortable. When a pitcher and batter get ready to face each other, each has a ritual they usually follow. Some batters kick the dirt twice or tug on their sleeve. Pitchers may hold the ball behind their back or push it deep into their glove. Batters waiting for a pitch may wave the bat over their heads or gently rest it on their shoulders. Pitchers may twirl the ball in their hands while looking in for a sign; batters may tighten their batting gloves between each pitch. These rituals, done before every pitch, can help both the batter and the pitcher calm down and get ready to do what they have done so many times before, and then go ahead and do it the same way again. By following the same rituals and routines before every pitch, pitchers and batters hope to block out the noise from the fans, the pressure of the count, or the number of runners on base. The rituals tell their brains, "This is just another pitch, like all the ones you've hit or pitched before. You've got this."

Problems, pressure, and the noise of life can throw you off your game. Hard times often require new ways of handling problems. But you can find comfort and confidence in your routines and rituals. As you get ready to face new and difficult problems, kick the dirt a few times. Rely on routines that calm and steady you before you act. Set up a regular nighttime routine, go to bed at about the same time every night, and get a good night's sleep. Take a shower to open your eyes in the morning. Spend time eating a healthy breakfast. Go over your plans for the day. Leave the house on time. Get help and advice from people you trust. These are rituals for the real world, routines that help you rise above the pressure and noise of the game. The problems may be new, but trust your old and reliable routines to get you through. It's just another pitch.

62

Deep Breath

A Calming Breath
A Good Night's Sleep

One of the most common and useful rituals for pitchers and batters is the deep breath, a calm moment of peace and quiet they take before every pitch. When the pressure, nerves, and noise in a big game build up, a deep breath helps players block out the outside world just long enough to focus on throwing a strike or putting the bat on the ball.

A deep breath helps you remember the answers on the big test and your lines for the school play. It calms your voice before you give a presentation to your class and relaxes your muscles before you touch the piano keyboard or sweep the bow across the cello strings. Your body even takes deep breaths on its own: a yawn is a deep breath that happens without you even thinking about it, filling your body's need for a short burst of extra air. Taking a deep breath at stressful times of your day refreshes you, calms you, focuses you, and prepares you for what you're about to do. That brief moment of peace and quiet can help you through many of life's stressful situations.

Your most relaxed and refreshing breaths come during sleep when your breathing slows and deepens. Young kids and teens need at least eight hours of sleep each night; some need ten. Your brain and body's ability to perform at the highest level depends on getting enough sleep. You will pitch faster, hit farther, and field better with eight hours of sleep. Your toughest classes in school will seem easier and your homework will go faster. You will be more creative and interesting, a better friend and teammate. Don't miss the chance to have a full night of deep breaths.

63

The Windup

Reach Your Full Potential

Most pitchers would rather pitch with a full windup than from standing still in the "stretch" position (see the next chapter). Pitchers' windups use the force from their whole body, twisting and lunging towards the batter, to launch the pitch faster and harder than they can with their arm motion alone from the "stretch."

Use all your talents and skills to be the best you can be. You may go far being a nice person, but you'll go even farther when you add energy and enthusiasm. You'll do well by being smart, but you'll do even better when you prepare and study. Looking good makes the right first impression, but then you make important next impressions by being someone people can depend on and trust. Reach your full potential by making the most of the strengths you have now and developing new strengths. Use everything you've got to launch yourself ahead.

64

Checking the Runner (the Stretch)

Limit the Damage

With runners on base, pitchers can't use their full windup motion because it takes longer to deliver the ball and makes it easier for baserunners to steal bases. Instead, pitchers stand straight up in the "stretch" position, first looking at the runner, and then quickly pitching without using more than their arm movement and a short step to the plate. The look over at runners on base "keeps them close," preventing them from taking too big a lead and making it harder for them to steal a base. Runners can't do harm if they're not allowed to move on to the next base. But if the pitcher is careless and forgets to check the runner or accidentally uses a full windup, bases are stolen, runs score, and the game can get quickly out of hand.

Most of the time, batters will get on base. How the game turns out depends on how far they get around the bases. Tricky situations in life can go quickly from bad to worse if you're careless and don't pay close attention. You can usually get over bombing one test, oversleeping one class, making one trip to the principal's office, forgetting one practice. But you must keep those runners in check, limiting the damage by not letting them move to the next base. If you're not paying attention to what has happened and to what could happen again, repeating the same mistakes, then problems will pile up and games can be lost.

65

Pickoffs

Accept Your Mistakes

If the fielding team doesn't get a batter out at the plate, the pitcher and fielders may try, try, try again. When runners get to base and take their lead, the pitcher can throw over to the runner's base *before* the next pitch, hoping to catch them off base. Or the catcher can throw to the runner's base *after* a pitch if the runner hasn't gotten back fast enough, a "backpick." If the runner is tagged out by the fielder covering the base, the runner has been "picked off" and is out. Pitchers and catchers love picking runners off—it fixes the mistakes that let the runner reach base in the first place. But pickoffs don't work very often. That doesn't stop pitchers from trying them, often more than once, each time a runner reaches base. But the more times pitchers or catchers throw over to the base, the more likely it is that one of their throws will get past their infielder, letting the runner happily move on to the next base.

You can't fix all your mistakes, and sometimes trying too hard to fix them causes more mistakes and more harm. Although you might feel bad about the way something you did turned out, trying too hard to fix it—especially in risky ways—can make things worse. Cheating on homework or on a test won't make up for not studying enough and will get you in bigger trouble. Telling more lies won't fix the first lie. Speeding on your bike to practice or a game is a dangerous way to make up time when you're running late. When you've already let the runner reach base, it's usually too late, and often too risky, to fix that mistake. Sometimes, you just have to accept you messed up, learn from what you did, and not make the problem worse by trying too hard to erase it.

66

Strikes and Balls

Consistency

The best pitchers are the ones who most consistently throw strikes. Fans, and sometimes even coaches, pay a lot of attention to the flashy and showy pitchers, the ones who throw the hardest or who have the trickiest breaking ball. But the pitchers who throw the most strikes usually get more batters out and win more games—even if their pitches don't get the *oohs* and *ahs* from the crowd.

Consistent beats fancy and flashy. Just ask the tortoise and the hare. Great performances that happen occasionally are thrilling, but it's the daily, weekly, monthly, and yearly consistent and solid performers who get good grades, good spots on their team, get into good colleges, and get good jobs. You should aim to be consistent, reliable, and steady rather than trying for short bursts of greatness. And when you become consistent, a surprising thing will happen—your good performances *will* become great over time. Consistent strikes will develop into consistent fastball strikes and consistent curveball strikes, and you'll be the pitcher getting the *oohs* and *ahs*. Your consistent, reliable performances off the field will earn kudos and admiration from all the fans cheering for you in the other aspects of your life.

67

Wild Pitches and Passed Balls

Missed Opportunities

Pitches that get away from the catcher often let runners move up to the next base or even score while the catcher fetches the ball. A wild pitch is so far off target the catcher may not even be able to put a glove on it. A passed ball is a pitch that a catcher could have caught but gets away instead. With runners on base, catchers must "be a wall," trying to block every pitch they can't cleanly catch so it stays in front of them and keeps the runners in place.

Life is full of missed opportunities. Although not every pitch is easy to catch, you should focus on preventing the important ones from passing you by. Of course, there will be some pitches too wild or difficult for you to "block" and they will get away from you. But when good opportunities present themselves, even if it seems hard to make them happen, be a wall and do your best not to let them get past you. You may not feel ready for the big audition, or you might be too busy for an after-school help session before the big test. Your youth group may be holding its annual volunteer event on a night you wanted to watch a big game on TV. You may have just found out about the deadline for applying to be a camp counselor the day before it's due. These are tough pitches to catch, but you never know when one of them could be a game changer, so do everything you can to not miss important opportunities.

68

Painting the Corners

Be Subtle and Polite

A skillful pitcher can throw to the corners of the plate where strikes are harder for the batter to hit than when they're thrown "right down the middle." Umpires aren't always very strict with their strike zones, meaning even pitches "off the corners" may be called strikes as long as they're not too far off. Strikes on the corners are less bold and direct than those thrown down the middle—and safer for the pitcher. By "painting" the corners with their pitches, pitchers get what they want—strikes and strikeouts—and lower the risk of giving up a big hit.

There are many situations in life where being subtle and polite is better than being loud and bold. A gentle approach often works best: nudging people in the right direction rather than shoving them there; guiding rather than forcing; hinting, not nagging. Temper tantrums don't work as well as calm and thoughtful discussions. Threats cause tension, while compromises comfort.

Giving commands and loud orders may make people resent you. Gentle suggestions show you respect others and will make them more likely to respect you. Politely ask for what you need rather than demanding it. Knowing how to paint the corners can make a big difference in what the batter does with your pitch.

69

Framing the Pitch

Help Others Look Good

The strike zone is small and landing a pitch there can be tough. Many pitches miss the strike zone, either purposely by pitchers ahead in the count or accidentally by pitchers off their mark. Too high or too low, inside or outside, catchers will "frame" the pitch, catching the ball while at the same moment sweeping their glove into the strike zone, trying to convince the umpire that the ball was there all the time.

See the best in people you care about, and "frame their pitches" so others also see them that way. Put them in the best light, boosting them up to feel better about themselves and look better to others. No one is perfect, but everyone has good qualities and has done good things you can focus on. If your sister applied to ten colleges and was turned down by six, tell the world about the four where she was accepted. If your brother didn't make varsity, help him feel proud about playing junior varsity—lots of people don't even try out. Help the important people in your life to not feel too bad about their mistakes and learn from them instead. Frame their pitches so everyone sees strikes.

70

The Fastball

Go with Your Strengths
Be Yourself

The fastball is most pitchers' "go-to" pitch, the one they throw when they really need a strike. Especially when pitchers are behind in the count, the fastball is usually their choice. The fastball is simple—no fancy arm motion or mysterious grip. Just rear back and throw the ball hard and straight, right over the plate. Although the batter may hit your best stuff, your fastball is usually still the right choice.

In life, when you really need a strike, you should go with your strengths and whatever has given you the best results in the past. Stick with what works, nothing fancy or mysterious. The good study habits that got you through the quizzes will get you through the big tests. The practice routines that prepared you for the short recital will also prepare you for the full concert.

Even if others tell you their way is easier or works better, be comfortable with who you are and confident with what you do well. Be yourself. Don't pretend to be someone you aren't just to please others. If you lose with your best stuff, you'll move on and try again. But usually, you'll win using your most direct and simple pitch, being who you are and doing what you do best.

71

The Changeup

Spontaneity

When pitchers have a good fastball, another pitch that comes in just a little slower, but otherwise looks just like their fastball, can be a very effective weapon. Batters adjust to a pitcher during an at-bat and from one at-bat to the next. When the pitcher can get the batter used to seeing fastballs and then throws a pitch that looks almost the same but travels slightly slower—the changeup—the results can be, well, striking. The batter swings for the pitch they expected, but the ball isn't there yet, and the swing is off target and way "ahead of the pitch," making the batter look silly.

Spontaneity means acting in a surprising or unexpected way. Spontaneity is life's changeup. As valuable as consistency can be, the occasional unexpected twist can add fun and a little excitement to your everyday routine. This is true in relationships with friends and family, and even just for your own fun. A change of pace, unexpected and spontaneous, can be refreshing for you and those around you. Clean your room without being asked. Plan a surprise party. Write a thank-you note. Do the extra-credit assignment. Do your laundry. Bring your mom flowers. Bring your dad flowers! Doing the safe and sure thing is good, but being too predictable can be boring. Be creative and clever. If all you throw are fastballs, the batters will quickly figure you out. Change it up once in a while.

72

The Curveball

Mood Swings
Get Help, You're Not Alone

The magic and mystery of the curveball is it starts out looking like one thing and ends up looking very different. When pitchers dramatically twist their arm and snap their elbow, the pitch drops from high to low and from one side of the plate to the other, confusing batters. Batters may swing at the pitch because it looks like a strike, but instead the ball dives to the ground before ever crossing the plate. Or batters may duck out of the way of a pitch that looks like it's going to hit them in the head, but instead they hear the umpire call "Strike!" as the ball breaks across the plate.

While curveballs on the mound may be effective, in real life they can be hurtful. When you start out looking like one person and end up acting like another, you may confuse and hurt those around you. Daily upsets, changes in your mood, and acting out can be part of growing up—but they can also be part of a more serious problem. If you react to upsetting things in your life by yelling at your parents and siblings, talking back to teachers, skipping school—those are all curveballs, hard for others to understand and deal with. When your mood is out of balance, your dramatic snaps and twists affect more than just you. Family who trusted you and friends who depended on you may be confused, hurt, and disappointed, and may duck out of the way.

If you are increasingly sad or angry, or feel the world has turned against you, don't throw curveballs at those who love and care about you. Instead, ask them for their help. They can guide you to counselors who deal with tough pitches all the time and will understand what you're going through. You're not in this alone.

73

The Pitchout

Obstacles in Your Way
Fears, Anxiety, and Insecurity

When the pitcher and catcher suspect a baserunner will be stealing on the next pitch, they may set up a plan to catch the runner with a pitchout. As pitchers begin their windup, the catchers will stand up tall and step out to the far opposite side of the batter's box from where the batter is standing. The pitcher throws the ball to the catcher, who then has a straight shot at throwing the runner out—no need to pop up from the crouch or worry too much about getting hit by a swinging bat. Nothing blocking their view or in the way of the throw, no obstacles. The pitchout is automatically called a ball by the umpire because the catcher receives the pitch so far from the strike zone. It only works when the pitcher is ahead in the count and another ball won't cause a walk or too big of an advantage in the count for the batter.

Obstacles are things that get in your way, and there are obstacles in the way of almost every goal you set for yourself. Usually, like when the pitcher is behind in the count with a runner on base and can't afford another ball, you must deal with those obstacles directly and can't avoid them with a pitchout. Rules, homework assignments, tests, short deadlines, stubborn people, computer crashes. No way to step out from the plate or get around those; just deal with them as quickly and as best you can so you can move on to the next step. But other obstacles *can* be avoided. Friends who have ideas that keep you from doing what you should be doing. Having the wrong supplies, books, or tools for the project you have to do. Distractions popping up on your screens. The TV or gaming device. Those are easy obstacles to get around. Call a pitchout. Step away so you have a clear view of where the ball comes from and where it must go.

Other obstacles come from inside of you and may be harder to step away from—being unsure about yourself or your abilities; worries, shyness, fear of change, or anxiety about what comes next. Or you may think you don't deserve to be doing what you're doing, that you're fooling people into thinking you're qualified, or that others in the same role would be better than you. The only way to move forward from any of these feelings of insecurity is to realize they are what's keeping you down. Be confident in yourself and in your abilities. You wouldn't be where you are today if you hadn't moved on from where you were yesterday. You belong here. The more you do anything, the better you'll be at it.

Step away from the obstacles of the safety and comfort you feel in your old ways and old habits. The worst that can happen if you take on a new challenge is you won't succeed, but you can always go back to the old way. You were only able to discover who and what make you comfortable *now* because you had the courage in the past to meet new people and try new things; imagine all the people you still haven't met, and all the things you still haven't tried that you might like even more. But don't wait too long in calling for the pitchout or you may fall behind in the count. If your fears, anxieties, or insecurities are too severe to rise up from, get help right away. Your parents, teachers, coaches, clergy, or a counselor can help you see yourself for the great person you are and help you stand up tall so you can make a strong throw with a straight shot at your target.

74

The Intentional Walk

Avoid Dangerous Situations

There are times in a game where batters are so much more dangerous at the plate than they would be as a runner on first base that the pitching team decides to purposely pitch four balls to walk them. By "pitching around" a good hitter, home runs may be avoided, and easier outs or double plays may be created on the base path. Making the wrong decision and pitching to this batter may lose the game. The four pitches during an intentional walk are not the typical balls that just miss the strike zone. Rather, they are thrown so far away from dangerous hitters they can't possibly reach them. If the pitch is accidentally too close to the batters, there's nothing stopping them from swinging and doing the harm the pitcher was hoping to prevent.

You know which situations in life are potentially the most dangerous and should be "pitched around," avoided to lower the risk. The wrong friends. The wrong advice from the wrong people. The wrong party. The wrong driver. Don't even get close to those; if you do, you may not be able to avoid them or the harm they can cause. Make the right decisions and intentionally walk away from things that may cost you the game.

75

Meetings on the Mound

Accepting Advice

When the game is going badly, or when the pitcher is facing a tough batter or has runners on base, the catcher, infielders, coach, or all of them together may gather on the mound to give advice and discuss strategy. Sometimes there are suggestions for the pitcher; other times the meeting is just to calm pitchers down and help them get their control and confidence back. The visit to the mound often leads to the pitcher throwing better pitches and more strikes.

It can be hard to see the big picture when you're standing in the middle of it. The tension and pressure of the game, with runners leading off base, batters staring you down, and fans screaming both for and against you, make it hard to perform your best. Let in others who care about you and listen to their advice. Your parents, teachers, coaches, and older siblings have experienced the same kind of situations and have also been in tough places. They understand what you're facing, how important—or not important—the issues troubling you really are, and how those issues fit into the bigger picture of your life. They also can advise you how best to react to the stress of the moment. If you welcome others to the mound and listen to what they have to say, you'll throw better pitches and more strikes.

76

The Pitch Count

Know Your Limits

The more pitches pitchers throw, the more tired their arms get and the worse their pitching usually becomes. Pitchers all have their limits, after which they risk the whole game and perhaps even their pitching careers. Throwing too many pitches can cause permanent damage to a pitcher's arm.

Know your own limits. Everyone has limits, both physical—how much their bodies can handle—and emotional—how they are feeling inside. Pushing yourself too hard trying to prove something to yourself or others can do permanent damage. People depending on you may also try to push you beyond your limits, hoping to squeeze out just another drop of your ability and skill, or a few more hours of your time and energy. Know when you are reaching your limits. This may mean turning down tempting chances to be a club officer, team captain, class representative, or volunteer leader. Being popular or getting honors and awards are not as important as your health. When your pitch count climbs too high, stop pitching. Protect yourself for the next game.

77

Relief Pitchers

No-Win Situations

Every game has two starting pitchers, but few games end with the same pitchers who started. Relief pitchers often come into the game when there's already trouble, with big-league pressure on their shoulders—runs in, runners on base, lots of walks, best hitters coming to the plate. Relievers can be expected, with only a brief warm-up, to shut down the other team's rally and get their own team off the field with as little harm done as possible. The high pressure changes everything; every pitch seems more important, every mistake feels more damaging. Even though it was the pitcher before who made the mess, the relief pitcher is expected to fix it. Relievers can do only so much. When they're brought into the game with the bases loaded and no outs, chances are runs will score.

You may be called in for relief off the field, too. One of the actors in the school play or one of the musicians in the school band gets sick and you're the backup. Even though you weren't the first choice for the play or the band, you should practice and prepare as if you have the starting role so if the time comes and you're called in, you'll be ates working with you on a group

k, but the project is due soon.

u were assigned to help a friend

eone at your after school job suddenly

l in for a few days or even longer. Relievers

many real-life games and should be prepared

called. But sometimes what you're asked to do may

able or even impossible. When the odds have piled up

you, your job becomes much harder. It's tough to come out

top in no-win situations. Do everything you can to save the day

– but go easy on yourself if it doesn't work out. Asking you to be a reliever, on the field or off, means people had faith you *might* be able to pull one out. If you can't, you may feel like you let everyone down— but really, you entered into a very difficult, no-win situation. Most importantly, don't be shaken or rattled. You'll be called into one of life's games again and you've got to believe in yourself so the next time you may beat the odds and win the no-win situation.

78

The Balk

Regain Your Confidence and Control

There are strict rules for how pitchers can and cannot move before they throw a pitch. Those rules protect a baserunner from being thrown out by a pitcher who fakes a pitch and then throws over to the base. If pitchers make a movement they're not allowed to, which is called a balk, baserunners get to automatically move up a base. A balk occurs with great drama—the umpire screams "Balk!!" in the middle of the pitcher's delivery. And umpires *always scream* when calling a balk. Pitchers are shaken by the scream; they then have to watch helplessly as each baserunner gets a free base. And then, the rattled pitcher must make another pitch! After a balk, the next pitches are often out of the strike zone and wild. Pitchers have trouble bouncing back from "balk shock," often leading to more damage than from the balk alone.

"Balk shock" is like many of life's unwelcome screams. In the middle of your daily routine, you may make a wrong move, and you hear "You're grounded!" "Pop quiz!" "Go to the principal's office!" "You're too late!" or "Not good enough!" Screams in life, even quiet screams, upset your plans, make you doubt yourself, mess up your rhythm, and throw you off your game. Your next move after the scream is likely to be wild and may cause more damage. When "balk shock" happens, remind yourself this is just one mistake in an otherwise well-pitched game. You made a wrong move and the runners moved up, but your next pitch is another chance to do it right. The best way to prevent another balk is to go back to your routine, to the movements that have been successful for you in the past. Limit the damage, get your confidence back, and take back control of the game. By doing that, the next time the umpire screams something when you're on the mound, it will be "Strike Three!!" as you've stepped up and gotten out of a tough spot.

79

Bases Loaded (Part 4)

Be Optimistic

Among the toughest times for a pitcher is when the bases are loaded. With all those runners on base, almost anything that happens next can score runs: a base hit, a walk, a passed ball, a wild pitch, a fly ball, and even a ground ball out. Pitchers often overreact to bases loaded by picturing all the bad things that can happen, and their pitches show it. Pitchers' arm motions change, they overthrow, or they aim; their usual go-to pitches miss their mark and runs score. But loaded bases also give the pitcher's team the most ways to get outs; force outs can be made at any base and double plays can end the inning.

When you're the pitcher and the bases are loaded, you can choose to be pessimistic, picturing all the bad things that can happen, or optimistic, imagining how things can turn out well. On the one hand, what happens next can be terrible; on the other hand, with the right bounce, things may end up just fine. Fearing the worst often leads to changing how you act in such a way that makes your fears come true. You can be too afraid, too shy, too nervous, or too worried about what may happen next. The math test will be hard and even though you studied hard, you might fail—or you might ace it! There are a lot of kids trying out for the school play and you may not get a part—or you might be the star! Tomorrow's forecast says snow so your school field trip may be canceled—or the forecast might be wrong and you'll have a great time! Be optimistic, not pessimistic. Imagine the best possible ending instead of the worst and don't overreact. You may end up being disappointed, but you will give yourself the best chance for ending the inning the way you hope. When you're the pitcher and bases are loaded, you've got them right where you want them.

80

The Perfect Game

Listen to Your Inner Voice

A pitcher's greatest achievement is to pitch an entire game without anyone reaching base—a *perfect* game. With a lot of strikeouts and fielding outs, the pitcher faces the other team's best hitters and worst hitters, switch-hitters and pinch hitters, and gets every single one of them out. Perfect games are very, very rare. In a perfect game, the pitcher makes all the right choices. With each new batter, and with each count on that batter, the pitcher must choose between fastball and changeup, curveball and slider, down the middle or on the corner, inside corner or outside corner, high or low. One wrong choice and the perfect game may be blown. Pitchers can't possibly make all those choices alone; they trust their catcher to co-pilot them. The catcher serves as pitchers' "inner voice," telling them which pitches are right, and which are wrong for each count and for each batter, moving the target, and framing the pitch. The perfect game is as much the catcher's great achievement as the pitcher's.

In your life, each day brings many choices you must make, one right after another. Some of the choices you make have little effect on the game, but others can make all the difference between winning and losing. The choices can be as simple as what to eat for breakfast and as hard as whether to join your friends in something you know none of you should be doing. Your inner voice, your conscience, is your best guide to the tough choices. You know what's right and what's wrong. You've been taught well by your parents and teachers; you have your own past experiences to learn from; you have seen what happens with the choices people around you have made. Listen to your conscience and pick your pitches carefully.

PART VI

EXTRA INNINGS

81

Home Field Advantage

Family

Every team would rather play on its home field. The well-known hills and holes in the outfield, the funny lumps and bumps in the infield, the familiar feel of the dugout, and the friendly faces on the bleachers all give the home team a big advantage over the visitors. Home teams also get to bat in the "bottom" of each inning, which means they have the last chance to score runs at the end of a game. Sometimes, it even seems as if the umpire's calls favor the home team. With the calm and comfort of home field advantage, teams almost always win more games at home than "on the road."

As life challenges and confuses you, take advantage of your home field. Your parents and siblings are your best friends, your most important teammates. At times it won't feel that way. You may think sharing a secret with your parents, or confessing something you're ashamed of to them, will only make things worse. It may feel like your siblings are ganging up against you. You may believe your friends at school care more about you, judge you less, understand you better, and certainly would never punish you. It is true parents can act more like umpires, and siblings can behave more like the other team. But that's just an act. An umpire doesn't worry about you, guide you, protect you or love you. The other team doesn't share life's experiences with you, trust you with secrets, or stick up for you during the toughest times. No matter how big the problem, how afraid you feel, or how terrible you imagine the outcome, your family is your ultimate home field advantage. You'll win many more games at home than on the road.

82

The Head Trip

Controlling Your Emotions
Controlling Your Temper

Emotions are the feelings we have inside of us. So many situations in a game affect players' minds and emotions, which can then affect their performance. Umpires' bad calls, walks, balks, hit batters, a close score, angry coaches, bases loaded, loud fans, and errors are among the many reasons players may feel stress. When the stressful events of the game are made even worse by the player's own emotional reactions, a "head trip" can happen. Players over-think, over-analyze, and don't forgive their own mistakes. The result is they worry more and play worse. They lose self-confidence, their temper flares, and they might even have a meltdown in front of everyone: stomping their feet, shaking nervously, slamming their bats, throwing their gloves. None of those reactions improves the way they play. Instead, they pile on and pile up, usually making the head-tripping players useless for the rest of the game. Entire big-league careers have ended for some players who couldn't control their head trips.

Your mind is very closely connected to your body, and your emotions have a big effect on your performance. When you let what's going on around you change how you feel about yourself and about your abilities, you become less effective. Rather than being your own worst critic, choose to be your own best supporter. Talk yourself up, not down. Tell yourself the situation isn't your fault or, if it is, the lessons you learn will help you do better next time. It may be the end of this game, but it isn't the end of the world. You will improve your game and get through tough situations in life if you can avoid the head trips. Head trips can end very badly, with lost games, lost seasons, lost futures—or you can end them before you let them start.

Even more important than controlling your swing or your pitches is controlling your temper. Losing your temper at others—or at yourself—may make you feel better for a few minutes, but it's very hard to snap back, regain your cool, and have others rely on you again. As much as you believe someone may deserve to see, hear, and feel your anger, the result of expressing it doesn't help you, them, or the rest of the team. Usually, your temper tantrum drives others away and makes it even harder to get what you want done. When you feel your temper rising, take a deep breath, talk yourself down and get back in the game. When you face a stressful situation in school—a test was harder than you expected, the teacher corrected you during a class discussion, or you're scolded for something that wasn't your fault— do your best to stay calm and stay confident. At home, your parents may blame you for something your brother did, your sister might take somethng that belongs to you, or a friend may say something that hurts your feelings. Any of those can send you into a head trip and cause you to lose your temper. You're going to make outs or errors in many real-life situations. What's important is how you handle them and what you do next.

83

The Umpire

Accept Responsibility
Follow the Rules

Being an umpire is tough. Deciding between balls and strikes, safe and out, fair and foul always pleases half the crowd and upsets the other half. The angry half always argues, very loudly, but umpires' calls never change. At least they get paid for the stress. For the players, blaming the umpire for the outcome of their at-bat, steal attempt, pitching performance, or for the outcome of the game itself, is as old a tradition as the games of baseball and softball themselves. It is true umpires sometimes make bad calls. Too often, though, players blame the umpires not because they made the wrong call, but rather because it's easier than blaming themselves for their own failures. For every called third strike or close call on the bases, it's not the umpire's fault if a batter didn't swing at a close pitch with two strikes or didn't slide when the throw was on the way.

The umpire's "bad calls" are like many of life's tough breaks, unlucky accidents, and bad coincidences. These are things you must live with and get over, because they don't change even if they're unfair or wrong. Umpires are human and they make human mistakes. More often, though, their calls are close enough to be right. To blame too much on the umpire ignores the obvious—if the play wasn't that close, it wouldn't have been up to the umpire. When the calls go against you in life, it is sometimes because you weren't a little more careful, a little more skillful, or a little luckier. It's tempting to find someone or something to blame. Blame the umpire. Blame your parents, teachers, siblings, teammates, or friends. Blame the weather, the time of day or the day of the week. But know it may be your fault; and even if not, blaming never fixes anything, and the people you blame may be hurt by your finger-pointing. Accept responsibility for your actions and for your mistakes. Still, other times, it's not your fault; a bad call just goes against you, and there's nothing more you could have done to prevent it. Umpires almost never change their calls. Move on.

Rules are rules, and it's the umpire's job to make sure players follow them. On the baseball and softball fields, at home, in school, and in the community, there are people whose job it is to make sure people follow the rules. As unfair as it may feel at times, you must respect rules and the people who apply them. Respecting the rules doesn't mean you can't respectfully discuss or even respectfully disagree. The key word is "respectfully." But the umpires in your life—your parents, teachers, the principal, coaches, the security guards at school—will almost always win. And, in most situations, that's what should happen. Rules are for the good of everyone playing the game, including you. Without rules, there would be no game.

84

Calling Time Out

Courtesy and Good Manners

The umpire must give permission to stop the game for any reason. Before a hitter steps out of the batter's box, or a coach walks to the mound, or a runner stands up from a slide to brush off and put their helmet back on, or a catcher runs out to talk to the pitcher, or a pinch runner enters the game, or even before an injured player can be helped, time out must be called. It's a very simple courtesy to follow, and the umpire usually gives time out when it's requested, so failing to ask for it makes you look bad and may even cause an out to be called on your team if, for example, you step off a base without getting permission first.

Courtesy and good manners are important in everything you do. Raising your hand to speak in class, saying "please" and "thank you," letting others talk without interrupting, asking to leave the room, holding the door open for someone behind you, or giving up your seat for someone who needs it more. These are simple courtesies to follow and others appreciate it, and admire you, when you do. But when you don't, it makes you look rude and selfish and it won't score points with the umpires in your life.

85

The Coach's Coaching

When You Need Better Advice

Coaches are just people, and their styles and approaches to coaching are as different as their personalities. Some coaches can seem scary and mean, others kind and giving. Some are loud and showy, others are calm and quiet. Some think they bring out the best in their players with praise, while others scold. Most times, their advice is helpful because they have been around and know a lot about the game. It's the coach's job to offer advice about how players can improve their game. Sometimes, though, their advice is not very helpful. It doesn't help a pitcher who can't find the strike zone for the coach to yell, "Just throw strikes!" After all, it's not as if the poor pitcher on the mound is *trying* to walk batters and only needs a friendly reminder that strikes are better. A batter stepping into the batter's box in the middle of a long hitting slump doesn't suddenly hit better when the coach screams, "I need you now, we just need a little hit." Unhelpful advice can hurt players. The harder pitchers try to throw strikes, the less likely they'll succeed. They start aiming and the ball bounces to the plate or flies over the catcher's head. The more batters press to get a hit, the more likely they'll swing at bad pitches and continue to slump.

Telling you the obvious when you're struggling makes you feel even more hopeless and helpless; unfortunately, it happens a lot. Your coaches, teachers, or even your parents may not realize you need help understanding *what* you're doing wrong and *how* to fix it, rather than just being reminded you're not doing a good job. Tips like "Make sure you follow through after you let go of the pitch," or "Throw it over the top, not from the side," or "Level out your swing," are useful and helpful suggestions for improvement. Be open to helpful advice from those who have been around and know a lot. Don't feel insulted or threatened by being told how you can improve—use the advice as a chance to grow, and as a challenge to become the best you can be. But when the suggestions aren't as specific and helpful, it's okay to ask the advice-givers—politely and respectfully—for real help. "What am I doing wrong, coach?" "What am I missing on this math problem, Ms. Jones?" "Mom, show me again how this tool works." Don't be too proud or stubborn to ask the coaches in life to better help you. They will appreciate you being willing and eager to learn, and that you value their opinion on how to do better.

86

The Coach's Signs

Follow Instructions
When Not to Follow Instructions

As the batter steps to the plate, or the runner on base starts their lead, players turn to look at the third-base coach. The coach goes through a series of hand signs and body touches that secretly code instructions to the batter and runner. Hidden among what can seem like weird or even funny movements are the coach's plans for the players—bunt, steal, "take" (don't swing), hit-and-run. Coaches are in charge, the leaders and brains of the team, directing the game from their "box" near third base. Bad things can happen when players miss a sign and don't properly complete their assignment.

It's important to see the signs and follow instructions. Even if you don't agree with the leader's instructions during a team or group activity, you need to follow them. The person put in charge is in that position because their experience and wisdom are greater than yours. If it turns out badly because you did what you were told, it's the coach's "fault," not yours. If, on the other hand, you *don't* follow the instructions and the play goes wrong, expect to be benched.

There are rare but important times when you should disobey the coach or another person in charge. If someone tells you to do something you know is wrong because it's dangerous, against your parents' or teachers' rules, or different from what you know is okay, you should refuse and report that person to your parents or to another adult you trust. Unfortunately, coaches, teachers, scout leaders, and other people you depend on occasionally take advantage of kids and do or say things they shouldn't. Your own sense of what's right and what's wrong must take over if that happens, and you need to get help right away, without worrying you'll get in trouble.

87

Thanks, Coach

Show Appreciation

At the end of the game, as teams are packing up and cleaning up, few players remember to thank their coach. Some coaches are paid; most volunteer their time. All appreciate being appreciated and thanked. Most even say, thank you back—and they smile when you've thanked them.

On the baseball and softball fields, at school, at home, and anywhere else people spend time and effort trying to help you, they deserve your appreciation. Your parents are your chauffeurs, chefs, first responders, and mentors; they love you for who you are, and prepare you for life. Your brothers and sisters share their experiences and offer their advice, even if you don't ask for it. Your teachers plan each lesson, grade each assignment, worry about what you've learned. Your doctor fixes what hurts. The bus driver greets you in the morning and afternoon and gets you to school and back safely. Your friends support you on your down days and make your up days more fun. Let those who help you know you appreciate them. Saying thanks is easy. Just one word, no practice needed. It takes only a second but watch the smile it brings.

88

Averages

Excellent Doesn't Mean Perfect

Of all the numbers and stats in baseball and softball, the most important are season averages. A batting average of .300 or more is excellent—that translates into at least three hits for every ten at bats. Another excellent average the big-leaguers use, a .400 on-base percentage, means you reach base safely (a hit, a walk, or getting hit by a pitch) four out of every ten trips to the plate. A pitcher's earned run average of 3.00 or less is also excellent—three runs or less allowed in a nine-inning game.

Excellent is different than perfect. If your batting average is .300, it means you *didn't* get a hit seven times out of ten. If your on-base percentage is .400, it means you *didn't* reach base six times out of ten. If your earned run average is 3.00, it means you *couldn't* prevent three earned runs each game. But all three averages mean you've done a great job. When you look back at your game and remember just one bad result, you're forgetting that the next time you try, you'll have another chance to improve your overall average. And it's the average that counts most, because it measures how well you've done and how steady and reliable you have been over the whole season. The low grade on your science test doesn't mean you're a bad student or even a bad science student. It just means you had a bad test. Your final science grade is based on more than one test, and the average of all your performances in all your classes means much more than just your science class. Every disappointing result is a chance to learn, a chance to be smarter and do better on your next at-bat, the next time you're on the mound or the next science test. While it's great to aim for being perfect, perfect is rare. Never be upset with just being excellent.

89

Practice

School

Ask any player or coach—games are more fun than practice. That's why they're called games! But your game performance can often depend on how you use your time at practice. Your muscles are trained with each practice swing of the bat, throw of the ball, and slide into base. Practice makes the talents you already have stronger, teaches you new tricks, and develops new skills. Without practice, your play is rusty, and your self-confidence can be shaken. Players who don't practice don't make the team; teams that don't practice don't win.

School is practice for life. Homework is practice. Studying for tests is practice. Classroom lessons are practice. The more you practice your school skills, the more you learn, the better your test scores, the stronger your grades, and the greater your achievements in life. The brain "muscles" you develop from homework, studying, and classroom learning are skills you'll need the rest of your life. Practice can be tough—on the baseball and softball fields, and in school. The workout is hard, the hour may be late, and your energy and enthusiasm can run low. But when you take the field for the next stage in your life, what you're practicing in school today will pay off. Without practice, your chances of winning are bad, and you may not even make the team.

90

Warming Up

A Final Review on Big Days

Warm-up before the game wakes up players' brains and muscles. Right before a game, players "loosen their arms," "get their gloves working," and "groove their swing." No matter how many hours of practice that week on *non-game* days, warm-ups on *game days* are very important. Otherwise, the wild throws, bobbled grounders, and awkward strikeouts remind the players when they're not warm, they're cold.

No matter how many times you've done something, and even if you just practiced yesterday, you start out cold each day. Give yourself "warm-up" time, a final review before all important tasks, tests, presentations, and performances. Warm-up should be as close to game time as possible so there's less time for you to get distracted after you've reviewed. Wake up an hour earlier on big test days to go over the material one more time. Get to the auditorium early for your concert and play your piece, or sing your scales, before the audience arrives. Go over your notes just ahead of the presentation to your class. With your last-minute review and warm-up, you focus and your brain's "muscles" wake up.

91

Handshakes

Building Bridges

At the end of every game, the competitors get together on the field before heading home. Each team lines up and walks past each other in a parade until every player on one team has said "Good game" to every player on the other team, and sealed it with a high five or handshake, a ritual celebrating sportsmanship and respect. When the two teams meet the next time, the rematch will be a more friendly one, hopefully, because the first game ended on good terms. That's called *building bridges*, which means making and keeping good relationships with others.

No matter how thrilling the win or how tough the loss, opponents should end the game by congratulating each other. Throughout your life, there will be rematches, times when your lives cross off the field with those you've competed with for spelling bee, science fair, debate tournament, student council president, an honor in math or history, college admission, or a job. Those people you lost to will be back, as will those you beat. If you *burn* bridges by gloating or moping, it will make facing them next time even harder. On the other hand, by *building* bridges with those you've competed against, win or lose, you make your next meeting with them more friendly and more enjoyable. You may even find yourselves on the same team someday, because opponents who show each other respect may become good friends, neighbors, classmates, or colleagues.

92

Dragging the Field,
Cleaning the Dugout

Clean Up Your Messes
Take Pride in Your Spaces

At the end of each game, the field shows wear and tear. Big holes around home plate and on the pitcher's mound, cleat marks, ruts and ridges on the infield—those should never be left for the next game. It is the job of the home team to immediately put the field back into playing shape. Even if it's a week until the next game and a tornado is in the forecast. Same with the dugout disaster: overflowing with power bar wrappers, empty energy drink bottles and used Band-Aids, to say nothing of the actual sports equipment, dugouts are cleaned corner to corner before going home. Ungroomed fields and dirty dugouts make the team and its players look bad.

Don't leave today's mess for someone else to clean up tomorrow. Don't even leave a mess for *you* to clean up tomorrow. And messes aren't just dishes in the sink, dirty laundry on the floor, or junk in the car. They include troubles or problems that are tough to face right now— like a disagreement with a friend or a question for your teacher about something you don't understand. Even though you may want to put those kinds of messes off for another day, you'll sleep better if you've taken care of them today. Tomorrow, after all, will come with its own new mess.

Pay particular attention to your personal dugouts—your bedroom, backyard, desk. Although no one else may have to share this mess with you, others see it and it makes you look bad. Your personal spaces are part of you, signs on the outside of who you are on the inside, like the clothes you wear and how you brush your hair. Take pride in showing the best dugout for your team and the other teams to see.

93

Injuries

Resilience
Sympathy

Although a famous movie quote says there's no crying in baseball, there is *plenty* of crying in baseball and softball. Injuries are common. They are caused by the ball, the bases, the ground, the bat, the cleats, and by the other players. Baseball and softball injuries can be serious, but most, thankfully, are mild and get better quickly. Most times, injured players can get right back up and "shake it off," earning the applause and admiration of those watching.

Along with the many joys of life, everyone has some disappointments. How you handle those is up to you. Resilience means being able to bounce back from disappointments, get right up and "shake it off." A bad test grade, a failed tryout, or even being grounded by your parents are disappointments. But if you can shake it off, learn from the experience, and bounce back, you are resilient and will earn the admiration of those around you.

Minor injuries may take you out of the game, hopefully for just an inning or two. While you're healing, think about others whose problems don't go away. Friends, classmates, and neighbors with disabilities and special needs may never get in the game. There are kids who are growing up poor and hungry. Use your short-term pain or weakness to understand the hurt and suffering of those who are always left sitting on the sidelines. Turn your hurt or disappointment into sympathy for those with greater needs than yours, and into action to help. Volunteer with Special Olympics; be a reading buddy to a friend or classmate with learning disabilities; make regular visits, and new friends, in a nursing home; be a "candy-striper" or playroom helper at a children's hospital; help an older neighbor with yard work; start a bake sale to raise money to "sponsor" a child in a poor country; serve food in a homeless shelter; collect used uniforms and sports equipment for kids who can't afford them. When you show sympathy for and help others whose needs are greater than yours, you'll feel better and heal faster, and so will they.

94

Superstitions

Believe in Yourself

Superstitions can be feelings people have about what will happen in the future and what they might do to change their luck. Baseball and softball players are a particularly superstitious bunch. They wear lucky underwear, don't wash their lucky socks, throw a lucky number of practice pitches, swing a lucky number of practice swings, count the sweat lines on their lucky hats, and never, ever step on those unlucky chalk lines. Superstitious players believe that by following their lucky habits and holding onto their lucky charms, good luck will find their dugout.

Belief is a powerful partner in everything you do. It brings you confidence and strength. If you strongly believe what you are doing is right and good, you will do it better. If you have doubts about your abilities or about the value of what you're doing, you will fail more often than you succeed. Stepping on the chalk line won't bring you bad luck—unless you believe it will. If you believe accidentally wearing the wrong socks will cause you to play poorly, your confidence will be shaken and your game may be, too. You have some control over every "lucky" or "unlucky" outcome. You can improve your luck by believing in yourself, in your abilities, and in what you're doing. And if that means wearing your lucky socks, either to the big game or the big test, go for it! But what happens if you can't find those socks on the big day? That's your chance to prove to yourself it's you and not the socks.

95

Spitting

Role Models

There is nothing about the games of baseball and softball that can possibly explain why players spend so much time spitting. Players spit before they hit and before they pitch, then again after they hit and after they pitch. When playing infield and when playing outfield. In the dugout, in the on-deck circle, in the bullpen. How did this habit develop, and why don't other sports with much more huffing and puffing than baseball spit as much? In the old days, ballplayers became spitters because of all the time they spent sitting around in the dugout chewing tobacco, one of the few bad habits missing from most other sports. Thankfully, there's a lot less tobacco these days, but spitting lives on.

Spitting is strong proof of the power of role models. Players who have never tried chewing tobacco spit sunflower seeds. Players who don't spit seeds just plain spit. They stuff as many pieces of chewing gum as they can fit in their cheeks to look like tobacco chewers. Unfortunately, there are many more habits and behaviors of "role models" that are equally disgusting as—and more dangerous than—spitting. Pick your role models carefully. The best athlete on TV may be the player you want to become on the ballfield, but may not be who you want to be off the field. The older kids at school may seem cool, but some of their habits and behaviors may be better to avoid than to imitate. Find the good habits and behaviors you like and respect in people, and model yourself after those qualities, but not necessarily after the people themselves—especially if they spit! Your best role model may turn out to be a combination of the best features of many important people in your life.

Remember also that others may be looking to *you* as a role model. How you behave, what you say, and what you do may guide those around you who look up to you. This is especially true of younger brothers and sisters who have close-up views of you and what you do. Act in ways you would want those who are watching you, learning from you, and liking you to act.

96

Genes

Make the Most of Who You Are
See the Inner Qualities of Others

Genes are the characteristics you inherit from your parents which make you who you are. Genes are what make your eyes brown or blue, your hair light or dark. The amazing differences in genes between people are obvious on baseball and softball fields. Players of the same age can be very, very different in size, speed, and strength. Those differences can change how the game turns out and can be what everyone is talking about in the bleachers. The biggest, fastest, and strongest players usually hit the ball farther, steal more bases, and throw the ball harder than the smaller and slower players. But while genes can make baseball and softball seem unfair or even cruel, genes can also be *beaten* by skills that have nothing to do with the physical gifts you inherited from your parents. Attitude, hustle, hard work, and lots of practice hitting, fielding, and pitching can be more important than genes in how you play.

Everyone is born with a different "package" of genes. Some packages are tall, fast, smart, and strong; others aren't. Those who succeed in baseball and softball—and in life—combine the package they were born with and the new skills they gain over time. Enthusiasm, how hard you try, how badly you want something, and how well you stick to your goals are all skills you can choose to develop. So are kindness, being generous and thoughtful, and having a winning personality. The package you're born with isn't a guarantee of success or an excuse for failure—it's only where your home plate is, where you start. How far you get around life's basepath will be up to you.

Look beyond a person's obvious "package" to find what they can contribute. Your shortest friends may be the fastest runners or the infielders with the best hands; or maybe they just are able to get on base more often because they have smaller strike zones. The clumsiest players on your team may be the most valuable teammates in the dugout because of their great attitude and sportsmanship. Your disabled classmate may be a great first base coach or team manager or official scorekeeper. Success in life, like success on the field, depends on a long list of contributions from people with different skills, abilities, and packages. The most important qualities of a person come from inside them. To see them and appreciate them, don't be blinded by anyone's outer package.

97

Rallies

Leadership

As depressing as being behind in a big game can be, rallying from behind to take over the lead is one of the most thrilling experiences a team can have. Players will remember a comeback win much longer than a win when they were leading all along. Each rally starts with a first step—a big hit, a patient walk, a daring stolen base. That step is followed by others, each building on the one before as the goal gets closer, until at last the winning run scores.

As teammates pile on the hero who had the last hit, walk, or steal to win the game, they'll also remember and congratulate the first player who began the rally. Leadership means stepping up when your team needs you. When it looks like all is lost and there's no chance of winning. Leadership means ignoring the odds and expectations. It means never quitting. Leaders find their inner strength, get over their inner fears, act on their strong beliefs, and find a way to get on base so others have the chance to follow. Every rally starts with a leader. A leader who knows that big things start with little things and leads by setting an example. Leadership off the field means standing up for what is right; defending others who are treated unfairly; being a friend to someone who needs one; showing your younger siblings the right way to behave; asking your parents how you can help them during busy or difficult times in your family. Everyone, regardless of where you are or what you're doing, will need to rally at times and every rally needs a leader.

98

Clutch or Clench

You're in Control
High Pressure

To come through in the clutch means to do well under pressure. The clutch hitter delivers the base hit when the game is on the line and there are runners on base. The clutch pitcher throws strikes, and strikeouts, with the bases loaded and the other team's best hitter at the plate. Clench is the opposite of clutch; it's what happens to a player who tightens up during tough situations and doesn't handle the pressure well.

The difference between clutch and clench is a matter of control. Do you control what's going on around you and how you react to it, or does what's going on around you control you? Clutch performers can block out the noise, ignore the baserunners, the score, and the screaming fans. They trust in their abilities and don't get distracted or upset by the roar around them. But players who clench let what's going on around them get the best of them, wiping out their talent, experience, and self-confidence. Will you be clutch, or will you clench? The answer may depend on whether you just *step* to the plate or *strut*

to the plate, on whether you *drag yourself* to the mound or *swagger* to the mound. When you get into a tough spot in your life, strut and swagger. It doesn't need to be obvious on the outside, but you should feel strut and swagger inside. You are the best of the best, the king of the mound, the boss at the plate. You are smarter and know more about what's going on than anyone else in the room. Your fingers own the piano, your singing is the sweetest in the choir, your speech wins the debate. Control the room, command the game, convince the crowd. Be clutch.

The need to do well under pressure is part of everyone's life at some time and, for some people, it happens a lot. Some people love high-pressure moments where they feel they are the only ones who can succeed in this situation because they are so clutch. Team captain, group leader, student council president, soloist in the concert. "Let me have the ball, coach!" Others clench at tense moments and dread high-pressure situations, so they tend to make their life decisions based on avoiding stress. Most people are somewhere in between: they would rather not be under pressure most of the time, but they usually can perform in the clutch when needed. Know yourself. You must work hard to do well, but you don't have to be under high pressure all the time or even most of the time. If you are happier being on the team, but not leading it, there's nothing wrong with that and it's an important thing to know about yourself. If you are not the kind of person who loves and lives for clutch moments, find paths in your life that don't demand such high pressure.

99

Streaks and Slumps

Balance Your Emotions

The flow of baseball and softball can affect each player and each team. Players may go through many games without a hit and then suddenly break through and start a weeks-long batting streak. Teams may win five games in a row, only to lose the next six. Each hit or win builds on itself, and so does each strikeout and loss. Baseball and softball flow through highs and lows. Teams who believe they are winners keep winning—until they lose. Then their confidence is shaken, and they can start to feel like losers. Hitters who keep failing think of themselves as failures until they get a hit or two—and then their confidence returns, and they feel like winners. But at the end of the season, the most *balanced* players and teams will be the most successful. Winning more than losing, hitting more than striking out—but without the big swings of streaks and slumps.

The worse a slump is, the better the streak that follows it feels. And, as thrilling as a streak may be, the next slump feels awful. Flowing between high peaks and low valleys in your life isn't good or healthy. Find balance. Learn to slow and level out the flow between the very high highs and the very low lows. Balance your emotions. No one is *always* a winner or *always* a loser. Some days will be better than others, some stuff in your life happier and some sadder. But don't let your flow carry you too high or too low. Even though you try to win most of the time, you will lose some of the time. And losing doesn't make you a loser. Finding balance can be hard. If you are having trouble leveling out your emotions, there are people around you who can help—your parents, teachers, school counselors, clergy. They've been through ups and downs, too.

100

A Game of Inches

*Stay Humble
When You Fail*

A pitch just slightly higher, a swing just slightly lower, a hit just slightly farther, a dive just slightly longer, a throw just slightly closer. Games are won and lost by inches of airspace that separate the champions from the runners-up. The winners almost never remember they came so very close to losing, but the losers always remember what might have been, had the inches gone in their favor.

Many good things in your life might have been bad things if not for the "inches" going your way. Be humble. Remember, without the right bounce, the right luck, and the right timing, someone other than you might have won. You should be proud of what you've done and happy for the congratulations that come with it, but never so proud you forget how close winning is to losing. Life is a game of inches. Being humble and polite when you win in life will help you handle a loss that may come tomorrow. But bragging and boasting will only make future disappointments feel even worse.

Failures also often occur by just inches. When you fail, don't lose perspective—and put losing *in* perspective. There may be very little separating you from the winners. Falling short this time doesn't predict how you will do in the future; it should encourage you to try even harder the next time. When an inch here or there can make the difference between being a champion or the runner-up, do everything in your power to get the extra inch. But not every inch is within your power to get. All you can do is try to control the things you have control over and keep trying until the ball bounces a few inches closer.

101

Heroes and Goats

*Celebrate Successes, Overcome
Disappointments
Manage Expectations*

Most teams have a couple of stars—players who seem to always hit the farthest, pitch the fastest, and field the best. But the stars are not always the heroes. In any one game, any player can become a hero. Players may become heroes by hitting home runs or pitching shutout innings. But often they become heroes with simpler and smaller things. They may walk or get hit by a pitch and force in their team's winning run. They may drive in the winning run with a bloop single or a ground ball that's misplayed for an error. They may come in from the bullpen just to retire the other team's last batter on an infield grounder for the final out. They may sprint home on a pitcher's wild pitch. Heroes' teammates pile on them and they go home with a giant smile, heroes for the day. But for every hero, there's also a goat: the pitcher who gave up the home run, walk, wild pitch, or bloop single; the fielder who made the error; the hitter who struck out with bases loaded. Goats' teammates may turn their eyes away and goats can go home in tears.

Today's hero is tomorrow's goat, and today's goat may be tomorrow's hero. Every game offers new chances for success and for failure; you may go from hero to goat overnight. Celebrate today's success, but remember it may have happened because of someone else's failure, or simply due to good luck. Be ready for tomorrow's disappointments when someone else becomes the hero because of what you did or didn't do. When that happens remember, if you keep playing, soon it will be your turn to be the hero again. And when your teammate, friend, or sibling is the goat because of something they did or didn't do that turned out badly, don't turn your eyes away. Support them, and remind them that their day to be a hero will come soon enough.

It can be tough being one of the stars on any team in life, because stars are expected to be heroes all the time. When stars become goats, as will happen once in a while, it can be harder to cope with because of everyone's (and your own) expectations. Just because you're talented and usually succeed, don't expect too much of yourself and don't be upset by what other people expect of you. You may have gotten the highest grades in math every year, been the top choice for DJ at every school dance, the employee of the month twice in a row at your summer job, or won the church essay contest every year you entered. But someday your streak will end. Think like the star player you are, but cut yourself some slack. Even stars fail, but true stars rise again.

THE GAME PLAN FOR PARENTS AND COACHES

Using These 101 Lessons in the Game of Life

We've shared with your kids and players 101 baseball and softball fundamentals and the myriad life lessons they can learn from those fundamentals. Collectively, these can help form a game plan for your kids' happiness and success in the major leagues of school, friendships, and family life. So, how does it all play out? Is there a crystal baseball or softball that can predict the future?

Our own kids grew up with these lessons and are now launched into their young adult lives. But we quickly learned that the lessons from the dugout don't age out just because kids step out of their childhood dugouts and onto the real adult diamond—the issues just get more complex. College, careers, marriage, mortgages, children of their own. Our kids continue to draw on the lessons from baseball and softball as they confront the challenges of their young adult lives.

Harley's son called not long ago to say he and his wife were ready to make a down payment on a clean-looking later model used car from a sincere-sounding dealer they met through an online listing. The car looked like a steal, and they were both so busy at work they just needed to quickly get wheels and move on to the next priority. All Harley had to say was, "Watch out for the hidden ball trick." His son remembered. They stepped back and spent a couple hours researching the car's history and checking out the dealer with the Better Business

Bureau. The car was a lemon, the dealer a lemonade salesman. Not a steal, no deal.

Another child, who was in graduate school at the time, contemplated adding yet another commitment to her already-overloaded schedule. It would be a worthy undertaking, but require a lot of time to do right. Harley and his wife asked her if she hadn't already reached her pitch count limit. Although it was flattering to be offered this big new role, if she overdid it, she could hurt herself and be out for the season. She declined the new opportunity in lieu of a few extra hours of sleep each week.

And when we suggested to yet another of the kids that he "throw the ball around the horn" after getting his first job offer out of college, he realized he needed to send thank-you notes to those who served as his references. Then we reminded him that if his new workday starts at 9:00 a.m., arriving at 9:10 is like swinging at the *second* pitch after the "hit-and-run" play is called—by then, it's too late.

Metaphor memories that last a lifetime.

Enjoy your kids' days in the dugout – they go by much too fast!

ABOUT THE AUTHORS

Photo credit: Sara Rotbart

Harley A. Rotbart, MD, is a nationally renowned pediatrician, parenting expert, speaker, educator, and writer. He has been named to Best Doctors in America for eighteen consecutive years, and is the author of more than two hundred medical and scientific publications, as well as six books for general audiences. He was a monthly contributor to *Parents Magazine* for more than six years, has written widely-read pieces for the *New York Times* and popular parenting blogs, and has made hundreds of media appearances. He coached youth sports for many years, from the little league through high school levels. On good days, he can still catch a pop fly and field a grounder.

Photo credit: Charles Wenzelberg

Ken Davidoff has been covering Major League Baseball for over thirty years. A former president of the Baseball Writers Association of America, he served as a baseball columnist for the *New York Post* from 2012 to 2022 and retains an emeritus status at *The Post*. He previously wrote for *Newsday* on

Long Island and *The Record* of New Jersey. Ken appeared regularly on The Major League Baseball Network, the YES Network, and Fox 5 New York. He now works as an adjunct professor at Endicott College in Beverly, Massachusetts, teaching writing and journalism courses. Ken has seen a major-league ballgame in fifty different venues.